"Love is one of the most popular theme
world. It is also one of the most misunderstood.
ing critique of the picture of a watered-down, self-centered, and all-inclusive (i.e., unholy) love that prevails in contemporary culture—and in too many churches. It is also a recovery of a God-centered picture of love in which God's love for the world is tied to God's holy love for his own glory. Only the latter makes sense of the gospel, and of church discipline. Any book that explains how God's authority and judgment are not the opposites of God's love, but rather its display, is radical—in the dual sense of recovering the root and offering prophetic critique—and this book is deserving of a serious hearing and a radical reception."

Kevin J. Vanhoozer, Research Professor of Systematic Theology, Trinity Evangelical Divinity School

"I don't know many people who have thought as long, as hard, and as well about the church as has Jonathan Leeman. He helps us to reconstruct our idea of the local church, not by rearranging the walls, but by refitting the two floorboards that undergird the church—love and authority. It seems our culture has been drawn to the former and rejected the latter because it has understood neither. In a world that is quick to react, Leeman challenges us to step back and reconsider love, authority, and the way they were designed to relate to each other. He opens our eyes to our hidden assumptions and fears about love and authority. With theological precision and pastoral sensitivity, he does much more than highlight our problems and fears—he also shows us a grand vision for the gospel working in the world through a church that rightly understands love, authority, and their inseparable connection. This is an excellent work for pastors, church members, and even people on the outside trying to make sense of what Christians believe. I am grateful that Jonathan has condensed his years of study about the church and pastoring in the church into such a potent book, and I'm excited for others to get their hands on this."

John Onwuchekwa, Pastor, Cornerstone Church, Atlanta, Georgia; author, *Prayer: How Praying Together Shapes the Church*

"In an age when authority is often undermined in the name of love, Leeman helpfully reminds us that love and authority are not opposites. Instead, he refreshes us with the biblical reality that love isn't defined by itself at all, but is defined by God. That also means that we cannot love our families, our churches, our neighbors, or our friends and leave God out of the picture. We love truly when we love for Christ's sake as we are brought into the orbit of God's love for himself."

Abigail Dodds, author, *(A)Typical Woman: Free, Whole, and Called in Christ*; contributor, desiringGod.org

"While multiple words can be used to describe the many strengths of Jonathan Leeman's new book, the word that most comes to my mind is *timely*. On the one hand, he clearly and cogently articulates how our culture has undermined the nature of God's love, especially in relation to the ideas of authority and judgment. On the other hand, he persuasively and passionately presents how the church of Jesus Christ, armed with a biblical view of God's love, can present to a needy world the goodness and beauty of God in multiple ways. Every church, with its pastors and people, needs to read this timely book."

Julius J. Kim, Dean of Students and Professor of Practical Theology, Westminster Seminary California

"The world does not understand divine love. Amazingly this is far too often also true of many Christians. Jonathan Leeman does a superb job in providing a biblically faithful and theologically rich study of this important teaching. I was personally helped to better appreciate this doctrine, and I am delighted in commending this book to others. You will be blessed."

Daniel L. Akin, President, Southeastern Baptist Theological Seminary

"In *The Rule of Love*, Jonathan Leeman skillfully demonstrates how a God-centered approach to love is far more satisfying and sustainable than our culture's fluid, anemic, me-centered approach. As it unpacks how God-centered love involves things like holiness, discipline, and authority, this concise book brings clarity to our cultural confusion and poses a timely challenge to the church: Will you display this love to the world?"

Brett McCracken, Senior Editor, The Gospel Coalition; author, *Uncomfortable: The Awkward and Essential Challenge of Christian Community*

"It is not only our society that is confused about what true love is and its proper relationship to authority, but also, sadly, the church. After perceptively diagnosing the condition of our culture, Jonathan Leeman offers a biblically and theologically faithful antidote to the distorted views of love and authority that we too often have embraced. Rightly grounded first in our triune God's holy love before moving to how love and authority function in the church, this book is a must-read if God's people are to recapture the beauty and glory of how our local churches ought to reflect God's love and authority before a watching world. My prayer and hope is that this book will be not only carefully read but also put into practice in our daily lives for the health of the church and the glory of our triune God."

Stephen J. Wellum, Professor of Christian Theology, The Southern Baptist Theological Seminary; author, *God the Son Incarnate*; *Kingdom through Covenant*; and *Christ from Beginning to End*

THE RULE OF LOVE

Other 9Marks Books

Church in Hard Places: How the Local Church Brings Life to the Poor and Needy, Mez McConnell and Mike McKinley (2016)

Why Trust the Bible?, Greg Gilbert (2015)

The Compelling Community: Where God's Power Makes a Church Attractive, Mark Dever and Jamie Dunlop (2015)

The Pastor and Counseling: The Basics of Shepherding Members in Need, Jeremy Pierre and Deepak Reju (2015)

Who Is Jesus?, Greg Gilbert (2015)

Nine Marks of a Healthy Church, 3rd edition, Mark Dever (2013)

Finding Faithful Elders and Deacons, Thabiti M. Anyabwile (2012)

Am I Really a Christian?, Mike McKinley (2011)

What Is the Gospel?, Greg Gilbert (2010)

Biblical Theology in the Life of the Church: A Guide for Ministry, Michael Lawrence (2010)

Church Planting Is for Wimps: How God Uses Messed-up People to Plant Ordinary Churches That Do Extraordinary Things, Mike McKinley (2010)

It Is Well: Expositions on Substitutionary Atonement, Mark Dever and Michael Lawrence (2010)

What Does God Want of Us Anyway? A Quick Overview of the Whole Bible, Mark Dever (2010)

The Church and the Surprising Offense of God's Love: Reintroducing the Doctrines of Church Membership and Discipline, Jonathan Leeman (2010)

What Is a Healthy Church Member?, Thabiti M. Anyabwile (2008)

12 Challenges Churches Face, Mark Dever (2008)

The Gospel and Personal Evangelism, Mark Dever (2007)

What Is a Healthy Church?, Mark Dever (2007)

Building Healthy Churches
Edited by Mark Dever and Jonathan Leeman

Prayer: How Praying Together Shapes the Church, John Onwuchekwa (2018)

Biblical Theology: How the Church Faithfully Teaches the Gospel, Nick Roark and Robert Cline (2018)

Missions: How the Local Church Goes Global, Andy Johnson (2017)

Conversion: How God Creates a People, Michael Lawrence (2017)

Discipling: How to Help Others Follow Jesus, Mark Dever (2016)

The Gospel: How the Church Portrays the Beauty of Christ, Ray Ortlund, (2014)

Expositional Preaching: How We Speak God's Word Today, David R. Helm (2014)

Evangelism: How the Whole Church Speaks of Jesus, J. Mack Stiles (2014)

Church Elders: How to Shepherd God's People Like Jesus, Jeramie Rinne (2014)

Sound Doctrine: How a Church Grows in the Love and Holiness of God, Bobby Jamieson (2013)

Church Membership: How the World Knows Who Represents Jesus, Jonathan Leeman (2012)

Church Discipline: How the Church Protects the Name of Jesus, Jonathan Leeman (2012)

THE RULE OF LOVE

How the Local Church Should Reflect God's Love and Authority

Jonathan Leeman

WHEATON, ILLINOIS

The Rule of Love: How the Local Church Should Reflect God's Love and Authority

Copyright © 2018 by Jonathan Leeman

Published by Crossway
1300 Crescent Street
Wheaton, Illinois 60187

All rights reserved. No part of this publication may be reproduced, stored in a retrieval system, or transmitted in any form by any means, electronic, mechanical, photocopy, recording, or otherwise, without the prior permission of the publisher, except as provided for by USA copyright law. Crossway® is a registered trademark in the United States of America.

Portions of this book have been adapted from my larger work *The Church and the Surprising Offense of God's Love: Reintroducing the Doctrines of Church Membership and Discipline* (Wheaton, IL: Crossway, 2010).

Cover design: Jeff Miller, Faceout Studios

Cover image: Shutterstock

First printing 2018

Printed in the United States of America

Unless otherwise indicated, Scripture quotations are from the ESV® Bible (The Holy Bible, English Standard Version®), copyright © 2001 by Crossway, a publishing ministry of Good News Publishers. Used by permission. All rights reserved.

Scripture references marked NIV are taken from The Holy Bible, New International Version®, NIV®. Copyright © 1973, 1978, 1984 by Biblica, Inc.™ Used by permission. All rights reserved worldwide.

All emphases in Scripture quotations have been added by the author.

Trade paperback ISBN: 978-1-4335-5963-1
ePub ISBN: 978-1-4335-5966-2
PDF ISBN: 978-1-4335-5964-8
Mobipocket ISBN: 978-1-4335-5965-5

Library of Congress Cataloging-in-Publication Data

Names: Leeman, Jonathan, 1973– author.
Title: The rule of love: how the local church should reflect God's love and authority / Jonathan Leeman; foreword by Mark Dever.
Description: Wheaton, Illinois: Crossway, [2018] | Includes bibliographical references and index.
Identifiers: LCCN 2018011964 (print) | LCCN 2018022875 (ebook) | ISBN 9781433559648 (pdf) | ISBN 9781433559655 (mobi) | ISBN 9781433559662 (epub) | ISBN 9781433559631 (tp)
Subjects: LCSH: Love—Religious aspects—Christianity. | Church—Authority. | Church—Marks.
Classification: LCC BV4639 (ebook) | LCC BV4639 .L3873 2018 (print) | DDC 231/.6—dc23
LC record available at https://lccn.loc.gov/2018011964

Crossway is a publishing ministry of Good News Publishers.

LB 28 27 26 25 24 23 22 21 20 19 18
15 14 13 12 11 10 9 8 7 6 5 4 3 2 1

To Alex Duke, Bobby Jamieson, and Ryan Townsend,
dear brothers and partners in the gospel

Contents

Series Preface

The 9Marks series of books is premised on two basic ideas. First, the local church is far more important to the Christian life than many Christians today perhaps realize.

Second, local churches grow in life and vitality as they organize their lives around God's Word. God speaks. Churches should listen and follow. It's that simple. When a church listens and follows, it begins to look like the One it is following. It reflects his love and holiness. It displays his glory. A church will look like him as it listens to him.

So our basic message to churches is, don't look to the best business practices or the latest styles; look to God. Start by listening to God's Word again.

Out of this overall project comes the 9Marks series of books. Some target pastors. Some target church members. Hopefully all will combine careful biblical examination, theological reflection, cultural consideration, corporate application, and even a bit of individual exhortation. The best Christian books are always both theological and practical.

It's our prayer that God will use this volume and the others to help prepare his bride, the church, with radiance and splendor for the day of his coming.

Introduction: When Love Is God

We got to let love rule.

—Lenny Kravitz

God is love, says Scripture. It's one of weightiest and most precious truths imaginable for a Christian.

God is love like oceans are wet and suns are hot. Love is essential, love is definitional, of God. His goodness is loving. His holiness is loving. His judgments are loving. His affections, motions, purposes, and persons are loving. Father, Son, and Spirit abide together purely and forever as love.

How sweet is that! The One who designed comets and acorns, who sustains our souls and bodies, who knows every one of our days before each comes to be—he is love.

Yet slow down. We need to think about what the Bible means here. When it says, "God is love" (1 John 4:8), it's not saying there is this thing out there called love and that God measures up to it. There is no dictionary definition of love hovering outside the universe, independent of God, so that God answers to it. Rather, God *in himself* provides the definition, the reality, of what love is. Love is not an abstract concept but a personal quality of God.

It's super important that you understand this. God's own character gives us the definition and standards of love. Dictionary writers should observe God and then draft their definition of *love* on that basis. Anything called love that does not have its source in God is not love.

Which means that understanding what love really is requires us to look at everything else about God—his holiness, his righteousness, his goodness, and so forth. God's righteousness, for instance, shapes his love, just as his love shapes his righteousness. The two are inseparable. Lose one and you lose the other.

Which also means that people today might say they love love, but if they reject God, they don't really love love.

Now, you and I could name dozens of romance movies and love songs popular today or yesterday. Love sells. Love is enticing. We devote a holiday to it every February, and our children give each other stale heart-shaped candies in celebration. Love is in the air and in the culture. But remember what I've said. Most fundamentally, love is not something independent of God but is a personal quality or characteristic of God. So to reject God is to reject that quality or characteristic, at least in part. We might think we love love, but rejecting God means it's something else we love.

Today you can justify pretty much anything by invoking the word *love*: "If they really love each other, then of course we should accept . . ." "If God is loving, then surely he wouldn't . . ." Yet notice what's happening in these statements. We're no longer interested in the God who is love. Rather, we're interested in our own ideas of love, which become god. "God is love" is traded in for "Love is god." Instead of going before the Creator of the universe and saying, "Tell us what *you* are like and how *you* define love," we start with our own views of love and deify them.

As a result, we harbor an idol hid in an utterly convincing costume, a lie no one can recognize, an angel of light. Love—or our notion of it—becomes the supreme justifier, boundary setter, and object of worship. That's what a god is and does.

So now we carry around something called love which possesses all the moral authority of God himself. The trouble is, it's not God. It's nothing more or less than our own desires—especially the desire to rule ourselves.

A "Love" Story

I read a love story in high school that popularizes this kind of costume. Generations of students have been shaped by it.

The story opens on a sunny summer's morning with five women gathered on a grassy plot outside a town jail. The date is unspecified, but it's sometime in the seventeenth century. The place is a small Puritan settlement in New England called Boston.

The action begins with a hard-featured woman of fifty offering counsel to four other women:

> Goodwives, I'll tell you a piece of my mind. It would clearly be for the public's benefit, if we women, being of mature age and church-members in good repute, should be given responsibility for handling a malefactress[1] like this Hester Prynne. What think ye, gossips? If the hussy stood up for judgment before us five, would she have come off with such a sentence as the worshipful magistrates have awarded? I think not.[2]

The so-called hussy, Hester Prynne, has committed adultery. The proof is the infant daughter cradled in her arms inside the jailhouse. On this particular morning, the town's magistrates have decided that Hester will emerge from her cell, proceed to the town scaffold, and receive several hours of public scorn for her sin. Along the way, and for the remainder of her days, she will be required to don an embroidered scarlet *A* on her chest. The *A* stands for *adulteress.*

The church is mortified, and the church's preacher, Reverend Dimmesdale, is aghast. A second woman explains, "People say that the Reverend Master Dimmesdale, her godly pastor, takes it very grievously to heart that such a scandal should have come on his congregation."

It's not just Hester's sin that scandalizes the church and the town. It's the fact that her illicit lover, the child's father, remains unknown. A hypocrite is at large, a hard fact to stomach in a "land where iniquity is searched out and punished in the sight of rulers and people."[3] Hester's refusal to reveal the father's identity doubles her guilt, and the gaggle of gossips wants blood. A third matron speaks: "The town magistrates are

1. A woman who violates the law.
2. This and the following quotations within the same conversation are taken from the edition of Nathanael Hawthorne, *The Scarlet Letter* that I read in high school (New York: Washington Square, 1972), 51–52. I have slightly modernized the language in several places.
3. Hawthorne, *Scarlet Letter*, 62.

God-fearing gentlemen, but too merciful. At the very least, they should have put the brand of a hot iron on Hester Prynne's forehead." Then a fourth: "This woman has brought shame upon us all, and ought to die. Is there no law for it? Truly, there is, both in the Scripture and in the statute-book."

I read Nathaniel Hawthorne's classic 1850 novel, *The Scarlet Letter*, in my junior-year English class. Perhaps you did too. The entire class was scandalized—not at the tragic heroine Hester but at the townsfolk. Did people like this really exist? We glared at them with all the disdain they poured onto Hester. How could they be so self-righteous, cruel, benighted?

Hawthorne's own sympathies in his story are hardly hidden. His descriptions of the five gossips make them look like gargoyles. This last woman he describes as "the ugliest as well as the most pitiless of these self-constituted judges." Compare this woman's portrait with Hawthorne's portrait of the woman she is attacking. The young Hester

> was tall, with a figure of perfect elegance on a large scale. She had dark and abundant hair, so glossy that it threw off the sunshine with a gleam, and a face which, besides being beautiful from regularity of feature and richness of complexion, had the impressiveness belonging to a marked brow and deep black eyes. . . . And never had Hester Prynne appeared more lady-like . . . than as she issued from the prison. Those who had before known her, and had expected to behold her dimmed and obscured by a disastrous cloud, were astonished, and even started to perceive how her beauty shone out, and made a halo of the misfortune and ignominy in which she was enveloped.

The contrast is clear. The reader can sympathize either with ugly and pitiless old women or with Hester's shining halo of beauty—not a tough choice for most people. Who wouldn't choose to sympathize with Hester? Employing a beautiful woman to "make the sale" is hardly an innovation of our marketing-hysterical age.

The reverend mentioned by the gossips, Arthur Dimmesdale, has a character of more complexity. It turns out that he's the secret scoundrel who impregnated Hester and left her to absorb the town's attack. Yet his character is more pitiful than malignant. He and Hester speak several times through the course of the book and at one point plan to run away and begin a new life together. Yet Arthur remains torn between his affections for her and society's hold upon him. Love pulls him in one direction; the Bible and the church, in the other. All but the most pitiless reader can't help but cheer for his liberation and their reconciliation. Ultimately, he is destroyed by the conflict between heart and mind, soul and society.

Hester's disgrace, ironically, frees her from church convention and social constraint. Never stingy with his symbolism, Hawthorne places her ramshackle shack outside civilization in the woods where witches and Indians abide, like the unclean Jew or Gentile dog outside the ancient Israelite camp. Yet it's out there, beyond the boundaries of respectability, that Hester is freed to love truly and divinely. She can forgive Arthur and her persecutors. She can dream of a different future with him. She can begin her career of caring for the community's poor. She can raise the sprightly daughter who will, in the novel's climactic moment, bend down to kiss her broken father's forehead. Hester and daughter almost shine like angels.

Assumptions about Love

If Hawthorne were living today, he might describe himself with the well-known mantra "spiritual, not religious." His fictionalized Puritan church codified every conceivable moral transgression and then handed these codes to the magistrate to be enforced. The problem was not the moral or spiritual impulse, Hawthorne would say. Spiritual impulses are good. The problem was placing these impulses inside a religious structure. The problem was institutionalization. Institutionalizing people's spiritual impulses is like covering flowers in concrete in order to protect them. See how long those flowers last.

It's worth noticing how Hawthorne managed to hit all of today's panic buttons: the church has subsumed the state; the private has become public; religious hate-mongers scorn the young, beautiful, and free. Even an innocent daughter is made a victim.

So just what kind of "love story" is *The Scarlet Letter*? It is one that well illustrates the assumptions about love that many people were beginning to make in the nineteenth century when Hawthorne wrote his book, assumptions that are foregone conclusions today.

Assumption 1. No moral boundaries or judgments can be placed on love. Rather, love establishes all the boundaries. You can justify anything by saying that it's loving or motivated by love. Heart plus heart equals marriage, teaches the bumper sticker. Love justifies extramarital affairs, divorce, fornication, cohabitation, depriving children of their biological (surrogate) mother in order to fulfill two men's dreams of being a family, never disciplining one's children, speaking dishonestly, and more.

Assumption 2. Love means unconditional acceptance and the end of judgment. Daytime television host Ellen DeGeneres had a guest on her show who describes herself as "nonbinary."[4] That means she refers to herself as "falling somewhere outside of the boxes of 'man' or 'woman.'" She wants to be known not as a *she* or *her* but as *they* or *them*. Ellen struggled with this language but finally concluded that love gives us our answer: we accept this woman's identity claim. "I think it's just about letting people be who they are and love who they want to love, and if you're not hurting anybody then there's nothing wrong with it."

Nathaniel Hawthorne never envisioned any of this, but there's a surprisingly short trip from *The Scarlet Letter* to a society's acceptance of a transgender movement. If love means unconditional acceptance, so that we should accept Hester's marital unfaithfulness, we should also accept a woman's claim, "God did *not* create me as a male or a female, but as something else."

Assumption 3. Love and authority have nothing to do with one another. Authority restrains. Love frees. Authority exploits. Love empowers. Authority steals life. Love saves life. This disassociation between love and authority is nothing new. They have been divided ever since the Serpent suggested to Adam and Eve that God's love and God's au-

4. "Ellen Meets Trailblazing Actor Asia Kate Dillon," March 19, 2017, https://www.ellentube.com/video/ellen-meets-trailblazing-actor-asia-kate-dillon.html.

thority could not coexist. Yet the contrast between love and authority came into even sharper relief with the Enlightenment and the Counter-Enlightenment Romantics.

Assumption 4. It follows that love is anti-institutional. Institutions, after all, impose authority on relationships. They are rule structures. In our minds, the words *love* and *institution* just don't fit together. Love helps relationships. Institutions hurt them.

This means we are inherently suspicious of everything in a church that smacks of institutionalism and authority. That includes talk about membership, discipline, offices, leadership structures, and so forth. Don't make me sign anything, please. Just let me show up, enjoy the show, sing, laugh, develop relationships organically, and head to lunch with whomever I want. Once or twice a year you can ask me to volunteer in a soup kitchen. I'll accept an annual dose of guilt. But please avoid words like *commit*, *covenant*, and *correct*. Those are legalistic and authoritarian.

Our Trouble with Authority

That brings us to the other topic of this book: authority. It's something that befuddles Westerners today. We don't like the idea of authority, as I was just saying, but our lives are suffused by it: hospital procedures, building codes, traffic laws, parental responsibilities, marriage covenants, student requirements, office rules, the laws of state, the grammar of language, the meaning of words, the rules of sports—on and on we could go.

Authority is the glue that enables people to live together. Apart from authority, all of life would be shaped by the preferences of the moment. There would be no traditions, no predictability of behavior, no stability of meaning, no shared morality.

Behind every authority structure, after all, is a moral claim. When we say, "You must do this" or "We must obey him," we are saying it's *right* to do so, and *wrong* not to. We are making a moral claim. "Honor your father and your mother," for instance, is the moral basis for the authority structure between parent and child.

The trouble is, we are a society that has destroyed its own ability to say "right" and "wrong." We have no moral vocabulary left beyond personal desire and identity. Which means it's nearly impossible with today's vocabulary to validate any claim to rightful authority. Even the authority of the state is typically grounded in every person's self-interest.

Yet how then do we organize our lives together? More crucially, how do we enjoy anything of transcendent value worth protecting over time? We protect something with *rules*. But how do we live as anything other than beasts whose only law is writ in tooth and claw? To decry all authority is to decry anything of transcendent value in human life. It is dehumanizing.

But if we do want to affirm the good of authority, who gets to say whose evaluations and structures are right? What if someone uses his or her evaluations and structures to oppress me? History offers a heartbreakingly long list of such abuses. One group of people creates a story—a particular telling of history—that enables them to rule over another group of people, exploiting them for personal gain. Reacting to such exploitation and abuse, we become anti-authority and anti-morality.

And yet, we cannot finally escape moral evaluation and authority structures. Even a society of angels abides within them. Life indeed is impossible without them, putting Westerners into an unresolvable bind.

The Local Church

Standing against all this, opposing the world's misconceptions of love and authority, is the divinely irksome while vaguely attractive local church. To the world, the church is both a fly in the ointment and the ointment. It spoils natural desires and inspires supernatural ones.

The world presumes to understand love and authority, like it presumes to understand God. Yet it understands these things only in their fallen forms, not in their created or redeemed forms. God, being gracious, has embedded in the hearts of humanity signs and symbols of true love and authority. Think of a wife's love of a husband or a father's rule over young children. Yet, at best, the world understands these things in a two-dimensional, shadowy way.

The local church serves, therefore, as a three-dimensional display of God's love and God's authority. No church is perfect, but there you begin to discover what God's love and rule are like. You receive his love and authority, experience them, learn them, even practice them. This living, breathing, and ordered collective called a church demonstrates love's demands and authority's blessings.

By God's design, the local church defines God's love and authority for the world. And it's both the relationships and the authority structures that do the work. In a biblical church, relationships and structures are inseparable, like a body and its skeleton, a game and its rules, a marriage and its vows. The love-defining life of a church depends specifically upon a structure we call a covenant, and is nourished through the oversight of elders or pastors.

Since Genesis 3 the world, the flesh, and the Devil have denied that love and authority belong together. But God's love draws lines. It puts up boundaries. It exercises authority. It makes commitments and offers corrections. Loving churches will do the same.

To be sure, churches can draw lines, exercise authority, and offer corrections unlovingly. They often have. But don't judge a gift by its abuses. Instruct and warn against the abuses, but then look to Scripture for guidance about the better way. It's crucial to keep one eye fixed on lessons from the fall to guard against misuses of authority. Yet we must cast another eye on lessons from creation and redemption.

Rethinking Love and Authority

This is a difficult message for our generation. On the one hand, we feel constrained to bow down and accept the morality and marital rights of all who say they do what they do for love's sake. On the other hand, we can view marital covenants as impositions on love. How much more, then, a church covenant? The idea of putting love and authority or love and binding commitments together clashes against some of our most basic intuitions.

Look at these verses from the apostle John, Christian. Do they make sense to you? Or do you have to tilt your head, gulp, and coach yourself, "Okay, I *suppose* this must be true"?

- "This is the love of God, that we keep his commandments" (1 John 5:3).
- "Whoever has my commandments and keeps them, he it is who loves me" (John 14:21).
- "If anyone loves me, he will keep my word" (John 14:23).
- "If you keep my commandments, you will abide in my love, just as I have kept my Father's commandments and abide in his love" (John 15:10).

The fact that such verses don't immediately make sense says something: our intuitions just might be malformed. Jesus, who spoke the last three verses, shows us what rightly formed intuitions sound like.

God is love, but God is also King. His authority is a gift; and his gift of authority to people, when used for its creational or redemptive purposes, is an action of love.

Mark Dever often reminds audiences of King David's last words:

> When one rules justly over men,
> ruling in the fear of God,
> he dawns on them like the morning light,
> like the sun shining forth on a cloudless morning,
> like rain that makes grass to sprout from the earth.
> (2 Sam. 23:3–4)

Good authority strengthens and grows. It nourishes and draws outs. You know this if you have ever had a selfless and loving parent, teacher, employer, coach, pastor.

The larger lesson of this book is that we need to learn anew what love and authority are, and what they have to do with each other. We need to re-form our intuitions. We need to remember something about love and rule that our ancestors in the garden forgot. For God, love and rule aren't two things but different aspects of one thing. Our culture has twisted our views of each, and therefore perverted both.

The main goal of this book, then, is to refashion our views of God's love and authority and their relationship together. I also have an ulterior goal: to suggest how the local church should embody these things. The church's gospel word, combined with its practices of membership and discipline, play a crucial role in defining and demonstrating love and authority for the world. The practices of membership and discipline in particular put the people of God on display, like a herald who pronounces, "Here are the people of God, the bride being made ready for her Bridegroom." They help the bride grow bit by bit in loveliness and glory.

While this book won't discuss the church at length, it will offer lessons for the church along the way. In a sense, this book is like a prequel or a prolegomena—a pre-word—to thinking about and living as the church. Many Christians today have a hard time grasping what the church is, because so many of our intuitions about love and authority are compromised. I hope to help us think better about love and authority, and then trace out a few lines for how that should impact our life together within churches.

Lastly, you will notice that I try to build a literary illustration or two into every chapter. If I wanted to sound responsible, I would say I did that because good literature reflects our society so well, as I believe *The Scarlet Letter* does. If I'm being a little more honest, I would say that the English major in me just wanted a chance to come out of the closet, run around, and have fun. Either way, I hope you find them useful.

1

Love in the Culture

Our ideas about love are more idolatrous than we realize. That was the introduction's basic point. We are less interested in the God who is love than in making our views of love god.

Later we will turn to how the Bible defines love, particularly in relation to authority. But first we need to get a better grasp of our idol. What shape does it take?

My own generation, which came of age in the 1980s and '90s, was inducted into the idolatry of love through romantic movies and love songs. The film *The Princess Bride* captured the vibe. It's a sarcastic fairy tale, but it's a fairy tale. Picture two blond and beautiful individuals, detached from all family and meaningful relations, alone in the world, beset by misfortune, yet trading ironic quips and saving themselves by the power of "true love."

Or maybe you saw the teen-bop romance movie *Say Anything*. If so, you remember the magical moment when the lead character holds a boom box above his head, arms outstretched, outside the second-story bedroom of the girl he loves—a Gen-X version of a damsel in distress needing rescue by her knight. She's restless in her room, imprisoned by an angry father. The music reverberates upward as the singer proclaims himself "complete in your eyes" in a way he could not be through "a thousand churches" and "fruitless searches."[1] The hero's message

1. Peter Gabriel, "In Your Eyes," side 2, track 1, on *So*, © Sony/ATV Music Publishing LLC, 1986.

couldn't be clearer: Our salvation is not in the church. It's in each other. We "complete" each other.

Sting, probably my favorite artist from that era, offered his own praise song to romantic love in the cut "Sacred Love," which says, "You're my religion . . . my church . . . the holy grail at the end of my search."[2]

Though these pop-culture references are dated, you can pick your generation—millennial, Xers, boomers, all the way back to the generation of *The Scarlet Letter* and before that—and each has its version of the same story. It's the story of individualism and individualist conceptions of love.

Individualism and Love

Love stories have existed for millennia. Yet, in the eighteenth, nineteenth, and twentieth centuries, a new conception of romantic love began to arise amid a flurry of poetry and novels.[3] Romanticism offered a vision of love decidedly set against the structures, heirarchies, and traditions of the past. According to this view, romantic love involves not just sexual attraction. It involves finding someone who "completes me."[4] It starts with looking inside myself: "Never mind father's expectations, mother's list of duties, or the vicar's sermons. Who am *I*, and what do *I* need? How do I feel about this other person? Does she understand me? Will she help me become everything I'm supposed to be?" Self-discovery then gives way to self-realization and expression: "*This* is who I am, father. I *will* pursue her."

On the American side of the Atlantic, one might think of *The Scarlet Letter*, where love defies the laws of religion, as we thought about in the introduction. Similarly, Jay Gatsby in *The Great Gatsby* tries to divorce himself from the past, rewrite who he is, and enjoy love with an upper-class married woman. His obsessive love battles not against religion but against the laws of old money and class. So it was in book after book on the British side of the pond, as with Emily Brontë's *Wuthering Heights* or the salacious work of D. H. Lawrence.

2. Sting, "Sacred Love," track 10, on *Sacred Love*, A&M, 2003.

3. Anthony Giddens, *Transforming Intimacy: Sexuality, Love and Eroticism in Modern Societies* (Palo Alto, CA: Stanford University Press, 1992), 39–40.

4. Giddens, *Transforming Intimacy*, 44–45.

The original Romantics were intentionally reacting against the cold rationalism of the Enlightenment. They wanted to be guided by love rather than structure, internal desire rather than external constraint, spontaneous impulse rather than rational deduction, beauty and freedom rather than efficiency and order. But they remained Enlightenment heirs. They were just as individualistic as those whom they reacted against. In the landscape of the novels, what matters is not who people are *in relation to their families or trades or religion*. These age-old structures don't define them. What matters is who they are *in themselves*—what they want, what they feel. Every relationship is a contract that can be ripped up. What's nonnegotiable is whatever my individual heart tells me is true.

Yet what is intentional in these older novels becomes unintentional and assumed in the popular films of my adolescence. Movie after movie presents handsome teenagers throwing off the oppressive hand of parents and teachers who "just don't get it." This is the story of *The Breakfast Club* and *Ferris Bueller's Day Off* and *Dead Poets Society* and *Dirty Dancing* and on and on. Each offers a vision of love that looks brave and attractive in its defiance. It is awake simultaneously to the inner self and to the mystical glory of love, like a soul in harmony with the cosmos. It courageously casts off all encumbrances in pursuit of its prize, while maintaining an impenetrable moral justification: "I act in the name of love." Who would dare go against that!

These days, our world seems to take this view of love—a love rooted in self-discovery and self-expression that justifies breaking every transgression—for granted. Over dinner, a friend who is my age said to me and my wife, "If two people really love each other, they should be able to be happy. We shouldn't stop them." I knew any direct challenge to her claim would be futile. The claim depended upon a set of moral intuitions developed in culture through decades and even centuries of morality tales. These intuitions were the unquestioned "of course" that needs no argument.

Notice how romantic love in this tradition becomes the perfect vehicle for sinful human beings to get everything they want: self-absorption *and* companionship; self-expression *and* moral approval; self-rule *and* the blessing of heaven; pleasure *and* an easy conscience.

Ironically, the individualist's love story becomes legalistic. Salvation belongs to those who follow the demands of romantic love. Opponents to anything called love are judged and vanquished. If you are a baker who refuses to bake a cake for a same-sex wedding, for instance, you might find yourself in court. If you are a high school student who says that sex, love, and marital commitment belong together, you will find yourself excommunicated from the circle of cool kids.

Yet Romanticism's priests will refuse to call it moralism. They call it pleasure and happiness. Their story culminates in a bed, after all, two lovers embracing one another, having cast off the world, enjoying all the delights of togetherness, staring into one another's eyes. The camera need not turn to parents or to children, as it never does in *The Princess Bride*. The couple is the center of the universe. It's Wesley and Princess Buttercup happily ever after, like in most romance movies. Could you ask for anything more?

Well, yes, in fact. The biblical teaching on love also includes a bed. But it places that bed in a garden, where the couple's union ultimately yields a flourishing world of rose bushes and apple orchards and a mess of children's shoes by the front door and swing-sets and skyscrapers. Biblical love creates a far, far bigger universe. It's not stagnant like a bed all by itself. It has forward motion and a story to follow. It's generative. It's fruitful.

Not only that, but the biblical story of love also makes more room for friendships. No one human being can meet all of another person's emotional, intellectual, and spiritual needs. C. S. Lewis wisely remarked: "In each of my friends there is something that only some other friend can fully bring out. By myself I am not large enough to call the whole man into activity; I want other lights than my own to show all his facets."[5] I often remind young married couples of this, particularly when they are jealous for one another's time. Wives should encourage their husbands to find good male friendship, and husbands should

5. C. S. Lewis, *The Four Loves* (New York: Harcourt Brace, 1960, 1988), 61.

encourage their wives to form healthy female friendships. We are happier and less demanding of our spouses when we don't ask them to play God for us.

Sure enough, every part of the body needs every other part, says Paul about the church (1 Corinthians 12). And how many parts does a body have? To truly experience love, we need far more than what a romantic partner can give us.

A brand of love that shines the spotlight exclusively on the couple, divorced from all other relationships, perhaps intentionally childless, perverts biblical love into something barren and stagnant. It's a universe that eventually collapses inward on itself. We might even say that Romanticism's story of love can't help but culminate in homosexuality, where a self seeks to complete and complement itself only in itself, its mirror image, two tabs colliding, two positively charged ends of two magnets, incapable of uniting or creating a new life. The rallying cry of "diversity" celebrates the ironic lack thereof in a same-sex partnership.

Biblical love, on the other hand, requires us to move out from ourselves. To draw toward someone different yet complementary. To forget ourselves temporarily and then discover ourselves more deeply. For instance, I am not a woman and I will never fully understand how it feels to be a woman. Yet God requires me to try by telling me to live with my wife in an understanding way. And so my mind must reach, stretch, lean forward in the attempt. I'm forced out of myself, my natural narcissism left behind. This might require self-denial in the beginning, which always looks painful beforehand, but ultimately I acquire a larger identity and a bigger world.

Consumerism and Love

Back to Wesley and Buttercup. If *The Princess Bride* were real life, we'd know their romance would eventually cool down.

Romantic individualism eventually gets worse. It grows shallow. Relationships are no longer fixed but negotiable, which means we identify ourselves less by whose son or daughter we are, or which village we come from, and more by our choices—like a shopper. The dreamy eyes of the romantic generation become consumer transactions in the next, and consumer transactions aren't usually guided by life's deeper spiritual or moral values. Increasingly, then, all of life becomes a shopping mall, and the individual's beliefs and values in that mall will depend on the appetites of the moment.

When we approach love and relationships as consumers, it's the more superficial traits that draw our attention, since the decision-making processes of a consumer rely on externals rather than on deeper, unseen qualities. Beauty counts more than character. Income more than constancy. Manners more than values. Sexual performance more than fidelity. What are you looking at in a store, after all: a label or an inner essence?

In the romantic love of the nineteenth century, sexuality was thought to emerge out of true love. By the time the sexual revolution occurred in the latter half of the twentieth century, good sex became a precondition of love. Sex became the test at the beginning of a relationship rather than a prize to be won deep into it. A greater emphasis fell on sexual skill and body type. Pornography found an easier market as the public became more easily duped by its fantasies.

With consumerism, happiness results from savvy purchases, and unhappiness and anxiety from poor purchases. The trouble, of course, is that no purchase really closes the deal. The possibility of buyer's remorse always looms. "Should I have purchased the other brand?" "Will a better model be released next month?" "What's the store's exchange policy?"

Consider then how the typical dating process works. A man evaluates his own purchasing power based on what he perceives is valued by women: personality, humor, stature, future prospects. Acting on this self-appraisal, he makes the best purchase he can according to whichever traits he most values in women: Intelligence? Beauty? Family background? In a market with ample supply, he can be more particular in his demands. It's not just beauty he's looking for; it's a particular body type. One sociologist writes, "Two persons thus fall in love when they feel they have found the best object available on the market, considering the limitations of their own exchange values."[6] We're more concerned about

6. Erich Fromm, *The Art of Loving* (New York: Harper & Row, 1989), 3.

who loves us, than we are about loving. And there's nothing to prompt a consumer to ask, am I desiring the right things?

An outgrowth of individualism and consumerism is a fear of making binding commitments. Sure enough, Americans today are less likely to join clubs, associations, and civic groups than their historical predecessors. We're marrying later and divorcing more often. We're also changing jobs and careers more often. Whenever a relationship becomes inconvenient or demands too much, it's left behind.

People today worship not just the god of love but the god of options. Individuals reach their late twenties and even thirties uncertain of what they want to be "when they grow up," so the experts give lectures on "delayed adolescence." How many men (including myself) have I counseled through the agonizing decision of whether to pursue this or that woman? After all, another woman could come along next month who's even better. Commitments bind us. Commitments are threatening. They are freedom curtailing. They are pleasure postponing.

As a result, the idea of commitment is removed from the ingredients of love. Parents justify their divorce because it's "most loving for the children." Higher percentages of couples cohabitate, claiming their love doesn't "need" a marriage license. Or, while they love each other today, "who knows about ten years from now?"

Yet stop and ask the cohabiting couple who in this present moment, really, are they most loving and protecting? Is it not themselves? Why else would they keep their future options open?

The love we idolize focuses on self-discovery, self-realization, self-expression. It focuses on externals. It looks for a bargain. It fixates on the present moment, divorcing the past and ignoring the future. It excuses itself when the going gets tough. It is, in all these ways and more, childish. It is also, in the final analysis, selfish.

Tribalism and Love

In recent decades, many people have reacted to the individualism of Western culture by emphasizing their group membership, particularly if that group has experienced injustice and oppression. Individualism and the political philosophy behind it, liberalism, are really just a mask for white male preferences, said a number of feminists and minority-rights theorists beginning at least as early as the 1960s. Our political institutions, these writers reasoned, need to give more attention to what it means to be female, or black, or Latino.

In general, the emphasis on group identity has helped bring the history of injustice and oppression against these groups to the forefront of today's political conversations. Exposing injustice is a good thing. Notice, though, that love in this conversation gets tied to the group. And this has risks and benefits. You are expected to show love for the group member not merely by regarding him or her as an individual. Instead, you affirm each member of that group as a sharer in the injustices done to that group.

Let me illustrate. Many whites pride themselves on being color blind. "I don't think of you as black. I just think of you as my friend." The black man might then understandably reply, "If you're my friend, you'll ask me what my experience has been like as a black man in this country." A friend once said that to me. He rightly identified a failure to love my friend well.

What such a reply also suggests is that it's easy for members of the majority like me to give preferences to our group but not realize it. Being in the majority allows you to treat your own cultural preferences as simply the norm or as objective, as natural as a fish in water.

Power disparities exist between different groups. And so love should account for the existential realities of group membership and injustice, particularly among the poor or downtrodden. Sometimes I wonder if, in the new heavens and earth, we'll discover that the saints who belonged to one oppressed group or another will find themselves ranked first, based on Jesus's promise that the last shall be first. And those of us who were first in this world will, on being ranked last, rejoice as much as any over the inversion.

Yet if individualism risks making the individual god, we can also make the group a god. Group identity, too, can be idolatrous. That's the implicit idea behind the label *tribalistic*. White supremacy is an obvious illustration. But there are many other forms. In general, we can say that group identity risks idolatry when I love the members of my group to the exclusion of other groups. I'm at risk when another person's group membership wholly determines my perspective on her, as if that were the most important thing about her and not the fact that she was created in God's image. I'm at risk when I forget what unites humanity and can only see what divides us. I'm at risk when I insist you love me on my group's terms. I'm at risk when I'm certain my tribe is always right and yours is always wrong, and I'm unwilling to listen to criticisms of my group.

My guess is that, in the history of the world, tribalism is the more common idolatry, not the idolatry of individualism. How many hatreds and battles and wars have been nourished in its soil!

When Such "Love" Infiltrates the Church

The local church should be the antidote to both individualism and tribalism, a place where each person stands individually before God *and* as a member of a new people and family. This new family doesn't smother the diversity of God's creation, or ignore the impact of this world's injustices and discriminations. God calls us to give greater honor to the parts of the body that have lacked it so that there may be no division (1 Cor. 12:25). Group diversity in a church is not a problem to be overcome. It's a gift to be welcomed, an opportunity for Christ's praise.

Yet what happens when Christians uproot individualistic or tribalistic love from the soil of the culture and transplant it in the church? When they sit in the pews and use the world's definition of love to judge whether or not a church is loving?

The Impact of Individualism and Consumerism

Let's start with the impact of individualistic love. When we love individualistically, the church becomes a place to grow in self-realization and self-expression. "Can I connect with the pastor? Does the music appeal to me emotionally?" We come, listen to the music, listen to the preaching, look around at the other people—"Do they look like me? Will I be comfortable with them?"—and then, on the drive home, offer an evaluation of everything we've seen: "I liked the music, except that one song. The preacher wasn't very funny. Did you see any programs for teenagers?" We rate our experience rather than search our hearts. We judge the church rather than letting God's Word judge us.

We score the church as "loving" if it makes us feel relaxed, comfortable, not judged. "I can be myself there." We're hypersensitive to the threat of judgment and quickly level the charge of "legalistic" anytime someone holds an opinion a little too strongly.

When love centers on self-discovery and expression, "worship wars," which pit the younger generation against the older generation, can be expected because it is through music that we express ourselves. The lyrics of songs will focus less on doctrinal content ("How firm a foundation, ye saints of the Lord, / is laid for your faith in his excellent Word") and more on expressions of emotion ("I could sing of your love forever, / I could sing of your love forever").

Sunday school classes, small groups, and other ministries will divide demographically because we become more intent on finding people who share our life experiences than on finding older people to learn from and younger people to disciple. Preaching becomes personal counseling on a group basis, as one early twentieth-century pastor put it. If asked about what we want in preaching, the first words out of our mouth are "I need something that meets me where I'm at," while the answer "I want it to be faithfully biblical" comes somewhere down the list, if at all. We won't admit this to ourselves, but what we really want from the preacher and small group leader isn't a God who asks us to make much of him, but a God who makes much of us. For that reason, short sermons are preferable in the main service, and dialogue is preferable in Sunday school or small group, centering on "what this passage means to me."

Spiritual-gift tests become popular when Christians view love as self-discovery and expression. Never mind where the church has needs. Never mind where the battle lines need shoring up. I need to feel fulfilled through my involvement at church. So let me tell you how God has gifted me personally, and then please assign me a position that allows me to express my own gift set.

What does consumeristic love look like in a church? It believes that size matters and that performance is what counts. Does the church put on a good show? A successful church service is one that produces a spiritual high or a mountain-top experience. Growth is counted through decisions made, not through "a long obedience in the same direction," to borrow a phrase. Statistics and other short-term measurements are all-important. We're no longer duped into worshiping carved figures, but statistical figures do impress us.

When the idea of a "binding commitment" is removed from the definition of love, churches become places where personal sacrifices are seldom made, and so the gospel is seldom pictured. Instead, individuals will come and go—"church hop"—with little care. We join lightly and we exit lightly, since doing so does not violate our sense of love and its obligations. We don't stop to weigh the consequences of our departure on others. We don't ask the pastors to help us think through our decisions. We take our purchase back to the checkout counter. It's nothing personal.

And so more and more Christians are not joining churches in the first place. The "experience provided by their church," says evangelical pollster George Barna, "seems flat. They are seeking a faith experience that is more robust and awe inspiring" than what the old local church can give them.[7] Barna himself is elated. Whether a Christian is "immersed in, minimally involved in, or completely disassociated from a local church is irrelevant to me (and, within boundaries, to God)," he says. "What matters is not whom you associate with (i.e. a local church), but who you are."[8] Remember, love is all about self-realization and connecting, and apparently churches aren't helping us along. Barna cites a number of statistics to make his point, such as the fact that eight out of ten believers "do not feel they have entered the presence of God, or experienced a connection with Him, during the worship service."[9]

The solution, for some Christians, is to get local churches out of the way. Take control of your own spiritual journey. For others, the solution is to find one of the new "boutique churches" that offer the "customized

7. George Barna, *Revolution* (Carol Stream, IL: Tyndale, 2005), 14.
8. Barna, *Revolution*, 29.
9. Barna, *Revolution*, 31.

experiences"[10] Americans are looking for. Either way, Christians can grow in maturity without all the hassles, bureaucracies, and redundancies of life in the traditional local church. The bottom line for Barna? You can take or leave church, depending on what suits you. You are your own spiritual portfolio manager. Your own captain. Your own shepherd.

When love becomes a matter of self-expression among Christians, the gospel itself—the very heart of Christian love—becomes refashioned for therapeutic purposes. We adopt what counselor David Powlison calls a therapeutic gospel. The therapeutic gospel isn't so much interested in how we have offended God in our sin. Rather, it focuses on how to heal from the offenses and abuses committed against us.

- I want to feel loved for who I am, to be pitied for what I've gone through, to feel intimately understood, to be accepted unconditionally;
- I want to experience a sense of personal significance and meaningfulness, to be successful in my career, to know my life matters, to have an impact;
- I want to gain self-esteem, to affirm that I am okay, to be able to assert my opinions and desires.[11]

The gospel and the church exist, describes Powlison, to solve problems like these. They should make us feel loved, significant, validated, entertained, and charged up. They address the symptoms. They don't so much tell us that our hearts are stone and that they need to be replaced. It's "jesus-for-Me." He meets my "individual desires and assuages my psychic aches."[12]

To be clear, I'm not calling for emotionally severe churches. I'm not saying Jesus doesn't heal our psychic aches and comfort the abused. I'm not even saying there is no truth in our culture's conception of romantic love. Reflections of it can be found in the pages of Scripture—just consider Song of Solomon. Rather, like all the best idols, our culture's understanding of love isolates one or two true things and makes those

---

10. Barna, *Revolution*, 63.
11. David Powlison, "The Therapeutic Gospel," 9 Marks (website), February 25, 2010, https://www.9marks.org/article/therapeutic-gospel/.
12. Powlison, "Therapeutic Gospel."

things ultimate, thereby distorting even the good in this view of love. So notice the emphases. And notice what it holds in highest regard and what it leaves to the side, like the authority and glory of God.

The Impact of Tribalistic Love

All of that is in answer to the question, how does individualistic and consumeristic love impact the church? What shall we say about the impact of a tribalistic love? In fact, it's much the same, especially in Western culture, where individualism suffuses everything, including our group identity. You can almost read through the paragraphs above and substitute the word *group* for the word *individual*. The church becomes a place to grow in *group*-realization and *group*-expression. We describe the church as "loving" if it makes *us* feel relaxed, comfortable, not judged. *We* can be *our*selves there. Preaching becomes *group* counseling on a group basis. *We* need something that meets *us* where *we* are.

The therapeutic gospel will play a significant role when a church is defined by tribalism, but, again, with the substitution of the *we*. We are less concerned about how to be right with God and more concerned with the validation of our group, our significance, our importance. Moreover, the gospel becomes focused almost exclusively on addressing the power relations between groups, either by maintaining the status quo (like the Pharisees of Jesus's day) or by upending it (like the zealots).

Again, let me be clear: when a group has been at the receiving end of injustice for decades or centuries, there *must* be a special measure of group acknowledgment, validation, and (to use Paul's word) honor. For an oppressed group to say "we matter" is simply to assert that they have been created in God's image, too, since the track record of oppression has called that very assertion into question. The risk I'm concerned with is when any group, majority or minority, becomes more interested in affirming its group identity than its Christian identity.

Rejecting Authority and Diminishing God

Lest there be any misunderstanding, the story of individualism, tribalism, and their versions of love isn't finally about the individual versus the community—being a loner versus having friends. It's about who's boss—me or someone else? It's about a rejection of all authority outside of *me*. And underneath that rejection of all authority outside of *me*, finally, is a disinterest in God's majesty and a belittling of his worth.

I am my own lord—lord of my life and lord of my loves.

If an institution, an authority figure, or even God stands in the way of what my heart wants, I possess the final trump card. I can say, "Out of my way!" That's what it means to say that every relationship, every cultural standard, every social and moral expectation, every religious creed has become negotiable.

"Individualism" and "consumerism" are tweed-jacketed sociologist's words. They serve their purpose just fine. But they are theologically neutered and a bit too "safe"—all horizontal and no vertical. Eventually we need to pull off their secular masks and talk about them as if we were sitting in our great-grandparents' Sunday school class, back when people used Bible words like *sin* and *greed* and *adultery* to name the bad stuff.

Not surprisingly, adultery played a growing role in the novels of the nineteenth and early twentieth century. Like teenagers who have grown suspicious of their parents' religion, a number of writers wanted to experiment and push the boundaries bit by bit. The shadows of moral compunction remained. These authors never came out and said, "Adultery is fine!" But everything else in the storylines pleaded for the reader's sympathy, like a voice whispering in your ear.

How many movies and books continue to do that today? I remember when the movie *The Bridges of Madison County*, with Clint Eastwood and Meryl Streep, was released in 1995. It was based on a 1992 book by the same title that was to become one of the best-selling books of the twentieth century at over sixty million copies sold. The storyline centers on an extramarital affair, and so when a friend told me she had seen and enjoyed it, I remember, even as a (then) nominal Christian, quietly condemning in my heart her lack of moral discernment. Yet for one reason or another I ending up seeing the movie and found myself—I admit with shame—sympathetic to the adulterous wife. The power of the storyline drew me in and deceived me.

How does transgressive, boundary-pushing art succeed in finding such large audiences? The artists behind it possess an "inside man" with readers or viewers—the fallen man inside of each of us. Authors don't try in ham-fisted fashion to convince us, say, that "adultery is good." Rather, they rely on the fact that our hearts desire to control our own destiny, as in, "If *your* heart felt that much desire, and *you* were encumbered by all those difficult circumstances, you would do the same thing, right?"

Temptation might knock on the front door with a bright shiny object in hand, but the Devil does his real work by first sneaking in through the back door and offering us a new identity: "You will be like God" (Gen. 3:5).

An individualistic view of love, finally, roots itself in a big view of ourselves and a diminished view of God. God might or might not deserve glory, but I certainly do. My impulses are good. My instincts are wise. My desires are reasonable and natural. I deserve what I want. I deserve praise. Therefore, I should define my own morality, my own existence, my own gender, my own love songs. God can offer a suggestion or two, but finally he has no right to rule me; nor does any parent, pastor, or president who tries to establish rules on his behalf. I know in my heart what love is. Who are you to deny love!

The tragedy, of course, is that such love doesn't finally generate or create. It remains stuck on itself and must eventually die.

By the first decades of the twentieth century, the novelists had concluded as much. Love, like war, is finally an exercise in futility, suggests Ernest Hemingway's *A Farewell to Arms*. Two lovers spend the novel running from the world so that they might be together. The woman gets pregnant. The man begins to wonder who he is. In the final pages, she dies in childbirth along with the child. He shoos the nurses out of the hospital room and turns out the light, wanting to say goodbye on his own. And yet, "It was like saying good-by to a statue. After a while I went out and left the hospital and walked back to the hotel in the rain."[13] The end.

13. Ernest Hemingway, *A Farewell to Arms*, Hemingway Library Edition (New York: Scribner, 2012), chap. 41, Kindle.

That's it. There's nothing more. Her love was all he had, and she died. So did their seed. Rain, a symbol of disintegration, washes all away.

The love of two lovers cannot sustain them forever, no matter how intense and passionate. This universe collapses on itself.

Tribalism, too, is fundamentally concerned with questions of power. As with individualism, it's disinterested in God's majesty but wants the group to be its own lord—lord of its life and loves.

Conclusion

Imagine two universes. In the one universe, God is on the throne. In the other, we are or our group is on the throne. In the first, God is the source of all love, and his love comes with his requirements. In the second, we are the source of love, and love bows to our demands. The Bible points to the first. The Western tradition of capital-R Romanticism, which has dramatically shaped our culture since the eighteenth and nineteenth centuries, effectively adopted the second.

Those are two pretty different universes. And the thing we spell *l-o-v-e* will behave pretty differently in those two universes. People will draw lines and boundaries in both universes. They will make rules and judgments. But those rules and judgments will look pretty different because they will serve different kinds of love.

In the final analysis, you cannot separate love and rule. It's only a question of which love will rule: the love of God, or the love of self?

2

Love among the Theologians

One of the more famous episodes in Fyodor Dostoyevsky's novel *The Brothers Karamazov* is the "The Grand Inquisitor." The episode is set in sixteenth-century Spain, in what the narrator describes as "the most dreadful period of the Inquisition, when bonfires glowed throughout the land every day to the glory of God." The Inquisition, just to remind you, was the Roman Catholic Church's multi-century investigation of heresy.

"The Grand Inquisitor" is a strange tale. It begins with Jesus quietly appearing on the streets of the city, not at his second coming but only "to visit his children for an instant." Everyone immediately recognizes Jesus and surrounds him. His "heart burns with love" for the people. He resumes the healing activity that marked his first ministry on earth. The people kiss the ground on which he walks. The children throw flowers and cry, "Hosanna." At one point, Jesus stops a funeral procession carrying the open coffin of a dead girl. He softly pronounces, "*Talitha cumi*," and the girl rises with smiling and astonished eyes. The crowd sobs in wonder.

Meanwhile, an aged observer stands back and assesses the scene. Seeing only commotion, the cardinal grand inquisitor himself, whose authority comes directly from the pope, intervenes and arrests Jesus. He later steps into Jesus's prison cell and challenges him:

> Is it you? You? . . . No, do not reply, keep silent. And in any case, what could you possibly say? I know only too well what you would say.

> And you have no right to add anything to what was said by you in former times. Why have you come to get in our way? For you have come to get in our way, and you yourself know it. But do you know what will happen tomorrow? . . . I shall find you guilty and burn you at the stake as the most wicked of heretics, and those same people who today kissed your feet will tomorrow at one wave of my hand rush to rake up the embers on your bonfire, do you know that? Yes, I dare say you do.

The grand inquisitor then reminds Jesus that he had given the church the authority to unite or exclude to itself whomever it pleased: "You gave your promises, you sealed it with your word, you gave us the right to bind and loose, and so of course you cannot even dream of taking that right from us now."[1]

The story ends both unexpectedly and, on reflection, expectedly. Christ, after being threatened with death, responds to the inquisitor's arguments with only a kiss on the mouth.

Like the inquisitor, we claim to find comfort in the fact that God is love. We talk of him. We wait for him. We prepare for his coming by building grand religious edifices. But when this God who is love comes, our fallen selves imprison, interrogate, and then kill him. The painter Rembrandt got it right when he painted himself into Christ's crucifixion scene as one of the crucifiers. Dostoyevsky's story is powerful for precisely this reason: it points to something deep in all of our hearts—a hatred not just for God but even for his love.

God's love simultaneously attracts and repels *all* of us. It's a thing of beauty and a thing of gross offense to the fallen heart. Gaze upon the love of God from one angle, and it will appear as the most resplendent thing in all the universe. But walk a few yards and look up again, and you will find that your lip snarls, your fists clench, and your heart becomes morally offended.

How can that be? In the first moment, we are the crowd, enjoying Jesus's healings and miracles and acts of compassion. In the second

1. Fyodor Dostoyevsky, *The Brothers Karamazov*, trans. David McDuff (New York: Penguin, 2003), 325–26, 328.

moment, we are the inquisitor, recognizing that Jesus's love calls us to surrender ourselves to his rule, praise, and glory. And our fallen hearts hate that, even in the face of mercy and love.

Like Wesley and Buttercup, we hold views of love revolving entirely around ourselves. Offense comes when God's love challenges our lordship and thirst for glory. So we redefine love to put ourselves at the center of the universe.

Chapter 1 concluded with a picture of two universes, one with us at the center and one with God at the center. And this picture is meant to convey the manner in which Western culture today challenges God. It aims at overt displacement. "Get off the throne, God. I deserve to sit there."

When we move inside the church, however, the challenge becomes subtler. We continue to honor his rule with our lips. We affirm that he's on the throne. But then we set about our lives as if *we* were his greatest love, and he loved us more than his Son, his righteousness, his glory.

Once again, picture two universes, but now with a slight twist. This time God is at the center of both, at least in name. What distinguishes these universes is what God most loves. In the first, he most loves humanity. In the second, God most loves God, as that love is shared between the three members of the Trinity—Father with Son with Spirit. Salvation in the first universe depends wholly upon God's love for humanity. "For God so loved the world" is the rallying cry. Salvation in the second depends upon God graciously including a people into his love for his Son, as when Jesus asks the Father to love his people with the same love he gives to Jesus (John 17:26).

These two universes will present a different set of rules, judgments, and loves. And that's what we want to consider in this chapter. If the last chapter explored the culture, this chapter explores Christian theologians. One group of theologians will talk about God's love as universal, undiscriminating, and unconditional, but at the core we find man-centeredness. Another group will talk about God's love as God-centered, and that's where the offense lies.

You may not think you're interested in the story of theologians, and a few things in this chapter might seem unfamiliar. But I suspect you'll identify with a few things as well.

Plato and Augustine

Let me start with a brief word on the Greek philosopher Plato, because of his impact on the way Christian theologians think about love. Plato used the Greek word *eros* for love. *Eros* or love for Plato was a longing for what we lack. It was desire. I behold some quality in you that I need, and I desire to be united to it. "I love you *because you are* beautiful" or "good" or "righteous" or whatever. Since the gods lack nothing, thought Plato, the gods must not love.[2]

Moving to Christian theologians, the fifth-century Augustine, like Plato, believed love begins with desire, mighty affection, or a "motion" of our soul toward some good.[3] And like Plato, Augustine believed that God lacks nothing. But unlike Plato, Augustine knew that "God is love" is based on the Scriptures. How did Augustine put all this together?

Augustine combined two things: love as desire (*eros*) and love as gift (*agapē*).[4] If love as desire sounds like, "I love you *because you are beautiful,*" love as gift sounds like, "I love you *because I want to do you good.*" The first depends on beholding some quality in the beloved. The second depends on the quality of benevolence in the lover. I assume you can identify with both. Love as desire, or *eros*, was your crush on that person in high school. Love as gift, or *agapē*, was that feeling you

2. Plato, "Symposium," in *The Collected Dialogues of Plato*, ed. Edith Hamilton and Huntington Cairns (Princeton, NJ: Princeton University Press, 1961), 533, 544, 553, 555 (secs. 178, 191, 200, 202).

3. For two very helpful discussions of Augustine on love, see Bernard V. Brady, "Augustine: Love God and Love All Things in God," in *Christian Love* (Washington, DC: Georgetown University Press, 2003), 77–124; and Lewis Ayres, "Augustine, Christology, and God as Love: An Introduction to the Homilies on 1 John," in *Nothing Greater, Nothing Better: Theological Essays on the Love of God*, ed. Kevin J. Vanhoozer (Grand Rapids, MI: Eerdmans, 2001), 67–93.

4. Augustine did not read Greek and so did not write in terms of *eros* and *agapē*. Generally, he used the Latin *caritas* (from which we get charity) as his word for love, but he would also use *amor*, more often associated with passionate love. Since his concept of love combined aspects of each, he denied their differences and said they could be used interchangeably. See Augustine, "The City of Gods against the Pagans," in *Cambridge Texts in the History of Political Thought*, ed. and trans. R. W. Dyson (Cambridge: Cambridge University Press, 1998), bk. 14, chap. 7.

had as a kid for your mom when you went Christmas shopping. You really wanted to bless her.

Augustine, again, combined these. God the Father bears a mighty affection (*eros*) for the Son through the Spirit, and gives himself to the Son entirely (*agapē*). Augustine named Father, Son, and Spirit as lover, what is loved, and love.[5] Likewise, God gives himself to us with the desires and affections of the Spirit, who then leads us to love and adore God passionately in return: "So it is God the Holy Spirit proceeding from God who fires man to the love of God and neighbor when he has been given to him, and he himself is love. Man has no capacity to love God except from God." For Augustine, in other words, love is a kind of boomerang, coming from God and returning to God, catching us up in its arced path. He writes, "Love therefore is God from God."[6]

I'm not aware of any place in which Augustine says that God most loves God in the way that Jonathan Edwards eventually would say it, but that's certainly the implication. He does explicitly say that human love, even love for other people and creation, should be given "with reference" to God. In a sermon, Augustine writes:

> You ought to love [your children and your wife] with reference to Christ, and take thought for them in reference to God, and in them love nothing but Christ, and hate it in your nearest and dearest if they don't want to have anything to do with Christ. Such, you see, is that divine sort of charity.[7]

We should love God for God's sake, and we should love our neighbors for God's sake. That means, quite simply, pointing our neighbor to God. Augustine writes, "Whoever, therefore, justly loves his neighbor should so act toward him that he also loves God with his whole heart, and his whole soul, and with his whole mind."[8]

5. Augustine, *The Trinity*, trans. Edmund Hill (New York: New City, 1991), 402 (15.10).

6. Augustine, *The Trinity*, 420 (15.31; cf. 15.32). Even if Augustine's formulation of the Trinity does depersonalize the Holy Spirit by reducing him to the love exchanged between divine Father and Son, as some argue, I believe we can at least affirm what Augustine says here; i.e., we may need to add to what Augustine says about the Spirit, but we don't need to take away.

7. In Brady, *Christian Love*, 117.

8. Augustine, *On Christian Doctrine*, trans. D. W. Robertson, Jr. (New York: Macmillan, 1958), 19 (1.22). Elsewhere Augustine says: "'Thou shalt love thy neighbor as thyself.' Now you love yourself suitably when you love God better than yourself. What, then, you aim at in yourself you must aim at

Love centered on anything other than God is the opposite of love: "If we love them for another reason, we hate them more than love them."[9] Summing all this up, Augustine writes:

> I call "charity" the motion of the soul toward the enjoyment of God for His own sake, and the enjoyment of one's self and of one's neighbor for the sake of God; but "cupidity" is a motion of the soul toward the enjoyment of one's self, one's neighbor, or any other corporal thing for the sake of something other than God.[10]

For Augustine, there are two basic kinds of love: a love centered on God and a love centered on anything else. One is from God and to God; the other is not. He clearly saw the two universes I've described, only he called them two cities. And there's a bright line in between them.

Bernard and Aquinas

In the twelfth century, Bernard of Clairvaux emphasized the experience of loving God more than Augustine did. Bernard used the imagery of romantic love and intoxication, from the Song of Solomon, to describe our experience of loving God.[11] Yet Bernard's general thrust is similar to Augustine's. God loves us by enabling us to love him: "He loves for no other purpose than to be loved, knowing that those who love him are blessed by their very love."[12] Do you see the boomerang of love arcing outward and then returning? For Bernard, love is its own reward. It's both give and take. God unites us to himself for himself, and in the uniting we receive everything we could want.

In the thirteenth century, Thomas Aquinas, like Augustine and Bernard, also conceived of love as coming from God and returning to God, again, like a boomerang. Aquinas too began with love as passion or desire and then combined it with a conception of love as gift, or desire for

in your neighbor, namely, that he may love God with a perfect affection. For you do not love him as yourself, unless you try to draw him to that good which you are yourself pursuing" (*On the Morals of the Catholic Church*, trans. Richard Stothart, in *St. Augustine: The Writings against the Manicheans and against the Donatists: Nicene and Post-Nicene Fathers of the Christian Church*, ed. Philip Schaff, vol. 4 [Whitefish, MT: Kessinger, n.d.], 55).

9. In Brady, *Christian Love*, 105.
10. Augustine, *On Christian Doctrine*, 88 (3.10.16).
11. Brady, *Christian Love*, 125–40.
12. In Brady, *Christian Love*, 129.

another's good. Love attracts one person to another and unites lover and beloved, but that uniting impulse carries with it a giving impulse. Love is like a furnace, Aquinas said, which radiates outward, bringing heat throughout a house. Hence, it's no good to say, "I love God but not my neighbor." Just as God's love burns outward for the world to bring people to the love and worship of him, so our love of God burns outward for sinners to bring them to God's love.[13]

Defining God-Centered Love

If we were to sum up what we've heard from Augustine, Bernard, and Aquinas, how would we define love? We would say true love is God-centered. It's loving others with respect to God. It's wanting another's good and knowing that that good is always God. He is the most glorious and beautiful thing in the universe. A God-centered view of love combines desire and gift. We most desire God, and we give God. It's like a win-win business proposition.

God-centered love works like a boomerang, starting with the Father's love for the Son and the Son returning that love to the Father. "You are my beloved Son; with you I am well pleased" (Mark 1:11; see also Heb. 1:9). So with sinful human beings, a God-centered love goes out from God and draws us into the arc of its path in order that our love might be returned to the thrower. He loves us so that we might love him. "For from him and through him and to him are all things. To him be glory forever" (Rom. 11:36), the apostle Paul says. True love is *from* God, *through* God, and *to* God.

A God-centered love is like a furnace in the heart—to use Aquinas's image—for the beauty of God wherever it's found. Simultaneously, a God-centered love hates all that opposes God, both because God is the greatest good and because such opposition lies about the good, defaming it. "Hatred of a person's evil is equivalent to love of his good," said Aquinas.[14] Only the irrationality of sin induces us to love what opposes God and not hate it. God alone is life and is worthy of praise. The forces of sin and evil oppose God and promise death.

13. Brady, *Christian Love*, 164–79, esp. 165–66, 171.
14. In Brady, *Christian Love*, 174.

Displaying God-Centered Love

For these purposes, a God-centered love draws lines between whoever loves God and whoever does not. It makes discriminations. It makes judgments. And it does so for the sake of loving God and the good of people.

This brings us to the storyline of God's people in Scripture. God marked off his people at every stage of redemptive history so that his love might be put on display. He drew a line between inside and outside of Eden, inside and outside the ark, inside and outside his people in Egypt through the plagues, inside and outside the camp, inside and outside the land of Canaan. And this same line should run around every church, marking off its members from the world.

The purpose of this drawing of lines is to say: "Here is a fountain of clean water; drink from it. Here are a people who love me with all their hearts, minds, souls, and strength. Do you see how attractive this blessed life is? Do you not want to repent and join them?" The line of exclusion means to provoke the desire for inclusion. It's a closed door, but it's a glass door that people can see through and open with the mere push of repentance and faith.

Yet these very lines, this display, and these doors are what offend the world about God's love. His love calls the world to love him, a call that by nature goes against the love of self. The lip snarls and the fists clench because self-love makes its own judgments, draws its own lines, cultivates its own hates. So Cain opposes Abel. Esau opposes Jacob. Pharaoh opposes Israel. And so the story goes, until the divine Son himself is destroyed by Herod and Pontius Pilate, fulfilling the rage of the nations (Acts 4:26–28).

This is why the grand inquisitor's hatred of Jesus is both surprising and makes sense. We can behold the beauty that is God incarnate, but then resist him utterly when he claims to possess us. You cannot serve two masters, Jesus said. You will either hate the one and love the other, or you will be devoted to one and despise the other (Matt. 6:24). And if we most love ourselves, how will we respond even to the beautiful and life-giving love of God?

From Luther to Barth

The story of theologians continues, however. The doctrine of Christian love evolved through church history, and the evolution was not altogether healthy. It's as if love in the Bible is a cord with multiple strands, and a number of later theologians have chosen one of those strands and isolated it from the others. This is crucial to observe because the isolated strand captures the way many Christians and post-Christians today view Christian love in its entirety.

Where Augustine and those who followed him combined love as desire (*eros*) and love as selfless gift (*agapē*), a tradition of theologians following Luther dropped *eros. Agapē* is Christian, they said. *Eros* is Platonic. Christian love is an unconditional gift. It is not interested in the worthiness or unworthiness of its object. In the process, however, these theologians prepared the way for swapping universes—exchanging a universe where God most loves God, for one where he most loves humanity. In effect, they prepared the way for God to become an idolater whose judgments would serve the glory of humanity, not his own.

As some tell the story, Martin Luther represents the turning point. Whether or not this emphasis characterized Luther's own writing about love or just the later interpretations of Luther is not our concern here.[15] But the story goes like this: The Roman Catholic Church emphasized man's work in salvation. Luther responded with the doctrine of justification by faith alone, by which God's justifying grace is freely promised to all who believe. In other words, Luther emphasized God's gracious and unconditional love for man—love as a selfless gift. Period.

One such later interpreter was Søren Kierkegaard, who made a strong distinction between Christian love and romantic love. Romantic love, Kierkegaard said, is specific. It focuses on "the favourite's name, the beloved, the friend, who is loved in distinction from the rest of the

15. This particular argument can be found in Anders Nygren, *Agape and Eros*, trans. Philip S. Watson (London: SPCK, 1982), 681ff. Nygren referred to Luther as ushering in a "Copernican Revolution" in the doctrine of love. It should be said that Luther's view on marital love included elements of attraction and passion. Whether his discussion of love in matters of soteriology emphasized God's love as a selfless gift, and whether Luther viewed God as doing all things for his own glory, I leave to the Luther experts.

world." Christian love, however, is universal. It never plays favorites but loves all humankind. Romantic love is "determined by its object." It's drawn in by attraction. Christian love is simply "determined by love." It depends on self-renunciation. It's a gift. Romantic love can be changed to something else, like hate. Christian love "is never changed, it has integrity; it loves—and never hates."[16]

As I said, I would guess many Christians maintain this kind of distinction in their minds between romantic love and Christian love. Yet what's striking is how often the Bible uses the one to symbolize the other. With ancient Israel, God describes himself as a jealous God, and Israel's unfaithfulness as adultery. With the church, he commands husbands to love their wives as Christ loves the church, and wives to submit to husbands like the church to Christ. No, I'm not saying that all love operates the same way in every domain. But could it be that God does not intend for us to pull romantic love and Christ's love as far apart as Kierkegaard did?

Following Kierkegaard was the twentieth-century Lutheran theologian Anders Nygren, who wrote an influential book titled *Agape and Eros*. Remember Plato and Augustine? Nygren wanted to separate Plato's idea of love as desire (*eros*) from a Christian idea of love as gift (*agapē*). A good portion of the book critiques Augustine for combining the two and commends Luther for pointing the church back to *agapē*. Nygren compares the two kinds of love in a series of couplets:

> Eros is acquisitive desire and longing.
>   Agape is sacrificial giving. . . .
> Eros is man's way to God.
>   Agape is God's way to man.
> Eros is man's effort: it assumes that man's salvation is his own work.
>   Agape is God's grace: salvation is the work of Divine love. . . .
> Eros is the will to get and possess which depends on want and need.
>   Agape is freedom in giving, which depends on wealth and plenty.

16. Søren Kierkegaard, *Works of Love*, trans. Howard Hong and Edna Hong (New York: Torchbooks, 1962), 36, 49, 63, 77.

> Eros is primarily man's love. . . .
>
> Agape is primarily God's love. . . .
>
> Eros is determined by the quality, the beauty and worth, of its object; it is not spontaneous, but "evoked," "motivated."
>
> Agape is sovereign in relation to its object, and is directed to both "the evil and the good"; it is spontaneous, "overflowing," "unmotivated."
>
> Eros recognizes value in its object—and loves it.
>
> Agape loves—and creates value in its object.[17]

For Nygren, love is completely cut off from attraction to an object. It's nothing but a self-sacrificing gift. It's never conditional but always unconditional. It's for the unworthy as well as the worthy, the sinful as well as the righteous.

Karl Barth can also be placed within this tradition. God is the "one who loves in freedom," says Barth. He loves as "an end in itself."[18] He loves for love's sake.

Today, some theologians have recaptured Luther's phrase "a theologian of the cross" and explicitly set themselves against a "theology of glory" (as Luther did). Among other emphases, they too deny that God's love has anything like desire or attraction in it; it's all a free gift.[19] Marilynne Robinson's novel *Gilead* provides this illustration as an old

---

17. Nygren, *Agape and Eros*, 210.

18. Karl Barth, *Church Dogmatics*, II.1, *The Doctrine of God: The Knowledge of God; The Reality of God*, ed. G. W. Bromiley and T. F. Torrance, trans. T. H. L. Parker and J. L. Haire (New York: T&T Clark, 2004), 279 (28.2.3). See also Miroslav Volf, *Free of Charge* (Grand Rapids, MI: Zondervan, 2005), 39. He explicitly builds on Barth and Luther on just these points. Those in the Augustinian and Reformed tradition might ask, "But doesn't God love for the sake of his glory?" Sort of, says Barth: "In loving us God wills His own glory and our salvation. But he does not love us because he wills this. He wills it for the sake of his love. . . . God loves because he loves; because this act is His being, His essence and His nature. He loves without and before realizing these purposes." In other words, he doesn't quite love for the sake of his glory. He loves us because he is loving; it's an end in itself. (Barth points to Deut. 7:8 and Jer. 31:3 to support these assertions.) But then, yes, he gets glory (and we get saved) because he's loving. God's love comes first; his glory and our salvation come second, as consequences of the fact that he loves. As with Kierkegaard and Nygren, Barth views God's love entirely as a gift; it's not given because of anything he beholds in the object of his love. Barth writes, "God's loving is concerned with a seeking and creation of fellowship without any reference to an existing aptitude or worthiness on the part of the love. God's love is not merely not conditioned by any reciprocity of love. It is also not conditioned by any worthiness to be loved on the part of the loved, by any existing capacity for union or fellowship on his [the loved one's] side" (*Church Dogmatics*, vol. II.1, 278 [28.2.2]).

19. For instance, Gerhard Forde writes, "This love of God that creates its object is contrasted absolutely with the love of humans. Human love is awakened by attraction to what pleases it. It must search to find its object and, one might add, will likely toss it aside when it tires of it" (Gerhard O. Forde, *On Being a Theologian of the Cross: Reflections on Luther's Heidelberg Disputation, 1518* [Grand Rapids, MI: Eerdmans, 1997], 113).

Congregationalist minister writes to his son: "Love is holy because it is like grace—the worthiness of its object is never really what matters."[20]

The Glory of God's Self-Giving Love

Readers may be surprised that I might have anything negative to say about this post-Luther tradition. Isn't unconditional love the highest form of love? Let me start by affirming what's right with that instinct. Self-giving, unconditional, *agapē* love is gloriously and wonderfully Christian. The idea here is biblical.[21]

What good news that is for us sinners!

Prior to God's loving us, none of us were intrinsically lovely. But God's love *creates* that which is lovely and valuable. That was true in creation, and it's true in redemption. In creation, God's "It is good" made us good because God's perspective on reality defines reality. In redemption, likewise, God's "They are righteous" makes us righteous in the way that matters most—from the perspective of his throne room.

It's the variety of love, we might say, that accompanies justification by grace alone through faith alone. It is good news for the despised things, the lowly things, the things that are not. It reaches out to thieves, murderers, tax collectors, and prostitutes.

God's love is a gift for the undeserving. Frederick Buechner, meditating on loving one's enemy, captured this idea sweetly: "And then there is the love for the enemy—love for the one who does not love you but mocks, threatens, and inflicts pain. The tortured's love for the torturer. This is God's love. It conquers the world."[22] Is such love not marvelous to behold?

Some Problems with *Agapē* Only

Ah, but there's the rub. It is attractive to behold. God's love for the sinfully unlovely is beautiful, and we *do* love God for such beauty, do we not? Paul even says that Christ's love "compels us" (2 Cor. 5:14 NIV). There is something in God's love that *attracts* us to God. Can we really

20. Marilynne Robinson, *Gilead* (New York: Farrar, Straus and Giroux, 2004), 209.

21. A number of words for love in the Bible overlap in meaning. None are technical terms, as if *agapē* always means unconditional, giving love. Context is key for determining meaning. Still, I will talk about *agapē* as Nygren and many Christians today use it.

22. Frederick Buechner, *The Magnificent Defeat* (New York: HarperCollins, 1985), 105.

say that the *agapē*-only view of love—love given apart from the worthiness of its object—is the highest or most godly form of love?

The divine Father does not love the divine Son with an *agapē*-only love. He utterly delights in the Son.[23] "This is my beloved Son, with whom I am well pleased," says the Father (Matt. 3:17). The Father sacrifices nothing to love the Son. He receives pleasure. And I don't think we want to say that the Father's love for the Son is a *lesser* kind of love, do we? Isn't it the foundation of all other love?

Christians don't love God with an *agapē*-only love. The opposite would seem to be the case:

> One thing have I asked of the Lord,
>   that will I seek after:
> that I may dwell in the house of the Lord
>   all the days of my life,
> to gaze upon the beauty of the Lord. (Ps. 27:4)

And aren't we to love like God loves?

It's not even clear that God loves sinners with an *agapē*-only love—"only for love's sake," as Barth put it. He loves them for the sake of his Son (John 17; Col. 1:18). He loves them so that they might become holy and blameless (Eph. 1:4–5). He loves them for the sake of his name and glory (Ezek. 36:22–23). He loves them to fulfill his covenantal promises and so prove that the Justifier is just (Rom. 3:25–26).

Theologians in the *agapē*-only tradition like to quote verses like Deuteronomy 7:8 ("it is because the Lord loves you") or Ephesians 2:4 ("because of the great love with which he loved us"). And we can say "yes and amen" to such verses. But doesn't the Bible say more, suggesting that love is a bit more complex than just that?

With *agapē*-only love, it wouldn't finally matter if sinners repented and turned to righteousness upon being saved. It wouldn't finally matter if they turned to worship the Son. It wouldn't finally matter if God's own standards of justice and righteousness were met. It wouldn't matter if people believed the right things. God doesn't open up our skulls and make

---

23. See Nygren, *Agape and Eros*, 678–80.

sure all the right doctrinal formulations are inside before he saves us, the thinking goes. God loves for love's sake.[24] One contemporary theologian has written, "God is an infinitely rich and most generous giver who receives nothing in return."[25] But is that right? Nothing in return? It's true he *needs* nothing in return, but he does *receive* praise and worship.

Here's the problem: repentance, holiness, and right belief are eventually cast to the side with *agapē*-only love. Such love softens or even dissolves doctrinal, ethical, and church boundaries. I dare say it's a crucial force behind liberal Christianity and has proven over the last century or so to be liberal Christianity's reigning ethic.

Think about it: what can I do if I want to call myself a Christian but also want to accommodate the culture's moral drift, particularly in matters of sexuality and family? Easy: I define God's love as a pure gift. Starting in the nineteenth century, liberal Christianity allowed professing Christians to accommodate what they believed a scientific worldview demanded by jettisoning Christianity's supernatural elements. Similarly, liberal Christianity has allowed Christians since the sexual revolution in the 1960s to accommodate changing morals by jettisoning Christianity's ethical elements. And an *agapē*-only view of love provides the perfect excuse: "God loves us no matter what!" It becomes the go-to excuse for a people, even for a nation, who likes the comfort of thinking itself "Christian" while adopting the moral standards of the world.

This is how so many Christians today talk and think. A recent news report, for instance, covered the story of a transgender high school sprinter, a freshman who, though born a male, won two girls state championships. The victory raised questions in the minds of some, but the sprinter's mother explained to reporters:

> I was raised as a Christian, and the concept around . . . accepting everybody was something I was raised with. . . . Being a parent means that it's unconditional, right? The love that you have for your child

24. As one would expect, proponents of pure *agapē* love want a transformed people in their theological system, as well. Nygren attempts to avoid cheap grace, for instance, by saying that God's love "demands unlimited devotion" (*Agape and Eros*, 104). But this sounds like an internal contradiction in Nygren. It would seem that something attracts God's love after all—the prospect of unlimited devotion!

25. Volf, *Free of Charge*, 37.

> is unconditional. And that means there's no judgment. There's no conditions around that. There's no ifs and thens. It's about all-encompassing love for your child.[26]

Insofar as our Christian intuitions have been cultivated inside the greenhouse of *agapē*-only love, it's difficult to know how to respond. All of our instincts want to say, "Well, yeah, I guess. Love does mean unconditional acceptance, right?" So if my son wants to call himself a girl and do women's track, shouldn't I accept him—or her?

Or we might listen to the rap artist Macklemore's song "Same Love," which commends homosexuality by quoting 1 Corinthians 13 over and over: "Love is patient, love is kind." This so-called Christian love becomes cover for justifying what God prohibits.

Using the same rationale, Christians leaders begin to blur the membership boundary between the inside and the outside of the church. At some deep intuitive level, member boundaries feel unloving to us. So leaders accept members into the church without asking questions about faith and repentance. Or they do away with membership altogether. As one author puts it, "The boundary between those who belong to the church and those who do not should not be drawn too sharply."[27] After all, "the establishment of clear boundaries is usually an act of violence."[28]

In an *agapē*-only view of Christian love, church discipline doesn't make any sense either. It might even be said to completely contradict our understanding of love and its demands. After all, isn't the gospel all about Jesus loving sinners? Why then would we remove someone from the church because he or she is sinning unrepentantly?

The problems here will become clearer when we consider the contrasting notion—God's God-centered love—more carefully in the next two chapters. But for now, let me tentatively suggest that love as *agapē* only is not big enough to accommodate all the dynamics of love in the Bible—all the strands that make up the cord. It picks one biblical strand and makes it ultimate. Without the other strands, furthermore, love

26. Dave Urbanski, "Transgender Freshman Sprinter, Born a Male, Wins Two Girls State Championships," theblaze (website), June 6, 2017, http://www.theblaze.com/news/2017/06/06/transgender-freshman-sprinter-born-a-male-wins-two-girls-state-championships/.

27. Miroslav Volf, *After Our Image* (Grand Rapids, MI: Eerdmans, 1998), 148n84.

28. Volf, *After Our Image*, 151n97.

becomes man-centered. It's little more than unconditional acceptance. "If you love someone, you accept who they are," says the daytime talk-show host. Yet affirmation and unconditional love are not the same thing.

In the final analysis, an *agapē*-only love yields doctrinal liberalism and ecclesial pragmatism. It envisions a universe where God loves man more than anything else, and therefore defers to man's terms.[29] It lurches toward universalism. It offers faith without repentance, which isn't really faith but mental assent. It extinguishes holiness and relativizes all morality. It has no choice but to capitulate to the standards of the present age. It undermines worship because it turns God into an idolater. Loving us appears to be God's highest and only purpose. Nothing else could be said to "attract" God. He becomes the servant of billions of gods—every human who has ever lived.

Now, I'm not saying that every theologian or believer who views love as *agapē* only takes these paths. I'm saying that this view of love pushes in these directions. It logically follows. Let Jesus walk around doing his miracles and raising the dead. But the moment he tries to take back control or draw clear lines between the church and the world, kill him.

Conclusion

Several years ago, a one-time pastor named Rob Bell wrote a book called *Love Wins*. It stirred up controversy in Christian circles because it effectively denied that people would go to hell. The message of God's eternal judgment, Bell said, is "misguided and toxic and ultimately subverts the contagious spread of Jesus' message of love, peace, forgiveness and joy that our world desperately needs to hear."[30]

Yet what does Bell mean by love? What is this love that will win? In Bell's mind, there is only one acceptable conclusion to the fate of every person who has ever lived: Most, if not all, will be saved. Most, if not all, will be forgiven.

---

29. Proponents of the *agapē*-only view explicitly argue that their definition is God-centered and that what came before was man-centered (e.g., Nygren, *Agape and Eros*, 681–84). I would agree, if we're talking about Rome's entire soteriological system versus Luther's. What concerns me is how love itself is defined.

30. Rob Bell, *Love Wins: A Book about Heaven, Hell, and the Fate of Every Person Who Ever Lived* (New York: Harper One, 2011), viii.

At an emotional level, I can understand the universalistic impulse and the desire for all to be saved. Eternal punishment is an emotionally difficult reality to embrace. Yet, notice how much Bell is like the grand inquisitor, asserting with moral indignation what he believes *must* be the case. "Has God created millions of people . . . who are going to spend eternity in anguish? Can God do this, or even allow this, and still claim to be a loving God?"[31] Bell knows better. He knows what love *really* demands. It *really* demands that everyone makes it out in the end.

Bell is, in effect, a hip and contemporary version of the grand inquisitor. He has rendered judgment over God, the universe, humanity, sin, and righteousness. He has, in his own head, determined what a right fate is for "every person who ever lived," as the title of his book implicitly boasts. And make no mistake, Bell, like the grand inquisitor, will crucify any God who does not conform to Bell. To the God who would send people to hell, Bell waves his hand like an exasperated king, "What kind of God is that?"[32]

Bells says love wins, but don't be fooled. His version of love wins only in a universe where we are at the center, not God. In fact, hate wins for Bell, too. He hates the glory of God.

So it is among all who insist that God loves us more than his own glory.

31. Bell, *Love Wins*, 2.
32. Bell, *Love Wins*, 3.

3

God's Love for God—Part 1

Cormac McCarthy's book *The Road* tells the story of a father and son's love for one another amidst a postapocalyptic world of ash and barrenness. Violent marauders often lurk just around the bend. Almost all of humanity has been decimated, though we never learn how or why. The story simply drops us onto a land of devastation with father and son traveling wearily southward toward the ocean. "Then they set out on the blacktop in the gunmetal light, shuffling through the ash, each the other's world entire."[1]

The father really is the "world entire" for the son. The son is too young to remember the world pre-apocalypse. He knows only what his father tells him, and interprets everything by the interpretations his father gives him.

The father spends the book sorting through old memories, his deceased wife, the boy's mother, especially. Yet loving and sustaining the son is now his sole purpose for living. Nothing else is left. All has been stripped away. The boy is his world entire, too. "He knew only that the child was his warrant. He said: if he is not the word of God[,] God never spoke."[2] Helping the son survive, in other words, was the father's one absolute.

I don't know if *The Road* would have emotionally registered for me had I read it before having children of my own. I remember looking down

1. Cormac McCarthy, *The Road* (New York: Vintage International, 2006), 6.
2. McCarthy, *Road*, 5.

at my first child, the first of four daughters, and feeling like my heart, overnight, had grown a new appendage out of my chest. It's different from your love for others because you know the child's existence has come from you. She didn't exist. And now she does. You and your spouse are uniquely responsible for her being. You are her world entire, and that elicits a deep and primal sense of responsibility.

For those who have never had a child, let me offer that the feeling you get when you first behold her or him, before the many inconveniences begin, is one of simultaneous self-forgetfulness and self-fulfillment. On the one hand, nothing else (in my experience, at least) produces such an immediate selfless love for another. It's like your joy sensors and fear sensors are no longer inside your body, but operating by radio wave from inside the tiny struggling thing lying on white hospital cloth. You only want what's good for her, what strengthens her, what protects and prospers her. Only a few days earlier, her existence, though inside a womb and real, still felt hypothetical. Yet now you feel certain you would die for this being if called to. And such a decision would seem easy, natural.

On the other hand, you don't vanish into pure nothingness, as with an *agapē*-only view of love. The word *selfless* isn't big enough to capture the love you feel, because the love's power roots in the fact that you see yourself in the child lying there. You don't feel this way for just any child. You feel it for *yours*. She is an extension of you. She bears your image and likeness. "When Adam had lived 130 years, he fathered a son in his own likeness, after his image, and named him Seth" (Gen. 5:3). Your very self is extended in the child, affirmed in the child, enlarged in the child.

In short, there is giving and receiving both.

These are not Christian instincts; they are human ones. God has programmed them, in varying measure, into all of us.

Why? Among other things so that we might know something about him. We need to be careful about taking any experience of human love and imposing that on God, but he has named himself "Father." He is its archetype (see Eph. 3:14–15). You don't finally need children to experience this, of course. Jesus never bore children of the flesh. But parenting is one tool God has hardwired into creation to give humanity a glimpse of his own love for the Son. You might just reflect on your parents' love. Or, if they loved you poorly, the hole they left tells you something. Why is there a hole?

Parental love, in a healthy form, doesn't fall neatly into the categories of giving or receiving, as if it were a zero-sum activity: more for you, less for me. Instead, it generates a win-win: more for you, more for me. As we will consider in a moment, parental love is, in that sense, like God's love and God's glory.

A Difficult Doctrine

In this chapter and the next I want to reflect on the love of the divine Father and incarnate Son for one another as revealed in Scripture.[3] This chapter is more biblical study. The next is more meditation on that study. Yet what we'll see in both is that God's love is like a boomerang, to continue the image from the last chapter. It is the original win-win as his love goes out and circles back.

But first, let me offer an umbrella claim that will cover everything which follows: the nature of love is complex. Parental love is different from romantic love, which is different from friendship love, which is different from love of ice cream. And inside each of these loves is a host of competing dynamics, even love of ice cream. I love ice cream, especially with chunks of brownies or cookies in it, but with some sadness in my heart I admit that it's possible to love ice cream too much.

Or we might think about how a husband who begins to stray from a marriage provokes his wife's jealousy, and how that jealousy, in right measure, is appropriate. A prodigal son, however, doesn't provoke the father's jealousy. Grief, yes, but not jealousy, per se. Romantic love and parental love are different.

In other words, love is not a one-size-fits-all thing, like a baseball hat with an elastic band. The different structures of different kinds of loving relationships require different ingredients, involve different duties, and produce different demands.

3. A fuller treatment should speak of the Spirit, too. But I will stick with Father and Son, since Scripture is most explicit about them.

New Testament scholar D. A. Carson points to the complexity of God's love with the surprising title of his book *The Difficult Doctrine of the Love of God*. The book argues that the doctrine of God's love is, well, difficult. Specifically, Carson traces out five different ways the Bible speaks of God's love:[4]

- *The peculiar love shared between the divine Father and Son*: "The Father loves the Son and has given all things into his hand" (John 3:35); "I do as the Father has commanded me, so that the world may know that I love the Father" (John 14:31).
- *God's providential love over creation*: the word *love* is not used in this connection, but he pronounces everything he has made as "good" (Gen. 1:4–31) and promises to send rain on the just and unjust alike (Matt. 5:45).
- *God's salvific love toward the fallen world*: "For God so loved the world, that he gave his only Son, that whoever believes in him should not perish but have eternal life" (John 3:16).
- *God's particular and elective love toward a chosen people*: "As it is written, 'Jacob I loved, but Esau I hated'" (Rom. 9:13).
- *God's conditional love toward his people based on obedience*: "Keep yourselves in the love of God" (Jude 21). "If you keep my commandments, you will abide in my love" (John 15:10).

Amid all this complexity, however, I maintain that there is a way to put it all together theologically—to sum it up, to systematize it in a concise definition. And what we learned in the last chapter from theologians like Augustine, Bernard, and Aquinas points us in the right direction by pointing to the God-centeredness of God's love. I'm not going to trace out all five of Carson's categories one by one, but in this chapter and the next two I will try to account for each, and then conclude chapter 5 with a definition.

We should start with the first and most important category: God the Father's love for God the Son.

4. D. A. Carson, *The Difficult Doctrine of the Love of God* (Wheaton, IL: Crossway, 2000), 16–21. Yet this insight is much older than Carson, going back at least to the post-Reformation. See Richard A. Muller, *Post-Reformation Reformed Dogmatics: The Rise and Development of Reformed Orthodoxy, ca. 1520 to ca. 1725*, vol. 3, *The Divine Essence and Attributes*, 2nd ed. (Grand Rapids, MI: Baker Academic, 2003).

The Love between the Divine Father and Son

Carson calls the love shared between the divine Father and the Son "peculiar." After all, the divine persons share one nature, one substance, one being, and one will. Humans don't do this, of course. The love shared between the Father and the Son (with the Spirit), then, is shared between three persons who completely interpenetrate one another, indwell one another, co-inhere within one another.

So whatever we might say about love between two people, it's not going to be exactly like the love shared between the divine Father and Son. Their love is utterly unique.

But don't walk out of the classroom just yet. The divine Son showed up as a man and said he wanted to teach us about love based on the love he shared with the Father. Somehow it could serve as an example for us. He said:

- He would love us *as* the Father loves him (John 15:9).
- We should love each other *as* he loves us (John 13:34–35).
- The love he shared with the Father could be *in* us (John 17:23).
- We should be one *as* he and the Father are one (John 17:11, 21, 22).

The Father and Son's love is unique. But the Son put on flesh and perfected the flesh so that we might learn about perfect love and imitate it.

So what do we learn about love from the Father's love for the Son? A number of things.

Love and Affection

First, we learn that love involves affirming and having affection for another—like *eros.* The Father loves the Son by affirming and delighting in the Son. At Jesus's baptism, the Father says, "This is my beloved Son, with whom I am well pleased" (Matt. 3:17). The word here for "beloved" comes from *agapē* (*agapētos*). The Father's *agapē* love for the Son is not a sacrifice for the Father. There is no self-denial in his love for the Son. Rather, it is filled with pleasure: "with you I am well pleased."[5]

5. See John Piper, "The Pleasure of God in His Son," in *The Pleasures of God: Meditations on God's Delight in Being God,* rev. ed. (Sisters, OR: Multnomah, 2000), 25–46.

The Father gives the same word of affirmation at the Son's transfiguration, when the Son's glory is revealed (Matt. 17:5). He is "well pleased" when beholding the Son's glory. He is "affected" by it. He enjoys it. He approves it.

In these ways, the Father's love for the Son reminds me of the old minister in Marilynne Robinson's *Gilead,* John Ames. Nearing death, Ames writes a letter to his seven-year-old son to be read when he's older. Ames says, "You see how it is godlike to love the *being* of someone. Your *existence* is a delight to us."[6] Likewise, the existence of Christ is a delight to the heavenly Father.

Love and Giving

Second, the Father's love for Christ teaches us that love involves giving. The Father loves the Son by giving all he has to the Son. It almost sounds like *agapē* love as we thought about it in the last chapter—love as a gift for another's good. The apostle Paul explains that in Christ "all the fullness of God was pleased to dwell" (Col. 1:19). Jesus himself testified that "the Father loves the Son and has given all things into his hand" (John 3:35); and "the Father loves the Son and shows him all that he himself is doing" (John 5:20). Even the fact that Jesus is "the image of the invisible God" and "the exact imprint of his nature" tells us that the Father has given him all (Col. 1:15; Heb. 1:3).

Somehow, the Father's love for the Son combines both love as affection or attraction and love as gift.

Meditating on these first two lessons more generally, we can say that love involves *attraction* and *affirmation,* and it involves *gift.* Start with attraction and affirmation: The high school boy sees a pretty girl on the other side of the classroom. The parent beholds the smile of a child. A wife enjoys the tenderness of her husband. In each case, a person sees something, is affected by it (has affection for), and affirms what he or she perceives. The person says, "Yes, you are worthy and good and worth my trouble." Then there's also a desire to give. It's not enough for the boy to see the girl and think she's attractive. That's just a crush. His soul will

6. Marilynne Robinson, *Gilead* (New York: Farrar, Straus and Giroux, 2004), 136; italics original.

need to desire her good and to aspire to work for her good. Godly, unselfish love wants to serve the object of love, help it, supply it, *give* to it.

Regarding the gift half of love, I appreciate the distinction one theologian makes between giving *of yourself* and giving *yourself*.[7] You might give *of yourself* with a lesser love. But you will give *yourself* with a greater love. The Father doesn't just give *of himself* to the Son; he gives *himself* to the Son. That is, he doesn't just give this or that part of himself, like his wisdom, his joy, or his goods, while keeping the better part of himself in reserve. Rather, he gives his whole self, so that Jesus can say, "I am in the Father and the Father is in me" (John 14:11), and "Whoever has seen me has seen the Father" (John 14:9). The Father gives himself to the point of identifying himself with Jesus, and the glory of the Father becomes the glory of the Son.

Love and Exalting

This brings us to a third lesson: we learn that love involves exalting another. The Father loved the Son by exalting the Son. "God has put all things in subjection under his feet" (1 Cor. 15:27). He established the Son as the head of a new creation so that "in everything he might be preeminent" (Col. 1:18). He gave him a "more excellent" name than he gave to the angels (Heb. 1:4). To none of the angels did the Father say, "You are my Son, / today I have begotten you" (v. 5), and "Let all God's angels worship him" (v. 6). Only to the Son did the divine Father say:

> Your throne, O God, is forever and ever,
>   the scepter of uprightness is the scepter of your kingdom.
> You have loved righteousness and hated wickedness;
> therefore God, your God, has anointed you
>   with the oil of gladness beyond your companions. (vv. 8–9)

The Father's love for the Son showed itself in his desire to see his Son glorified above all creation. That's why Jesus could pray, "Father, I desire that they also, whom you have given me, may be with me where

7. Jules Toner, *The Experience of Love* (Washington, DC: Corpus, 1968), 125, 127, cited in Bernard V. Brady, *Christian Love: How Christians through the Ages Have Understood Love* (Washington, DC: Georgetown University Press, 2003), 244–45.

I am, *to see my glory that you have given me because you loved me* before the foundation of the world" (John 17:24).

Let me see if I can bring this third idea down to earth by going back to my love for my daughters. Sometimes, I admit, it's tempting to feel jealous when others are exalted. Yet that temptation never arises in my heart with my daughters. If there is anyone on planet Earth for whom I would gladly get down on my hands and knees so that she might stand on my back and rule as queen, it would be any of my daughters.

Now, as we'll consider more in chapter 5, Christian love isn't finally about wanting other people to be exalted, but about wanting the Son exalted in them. But you get the gist. Love involves promoting another, even above yourself: "Count others more significant than yourselves" (Phil. 2:3).

Love and Obedience

Fourth, the relationship between God the Father and the incarnate Son teaches us about the relationship between love and obedience. And this is a lesson contemporary folk don't expect.

Again, we tend to think that the highest form of love is unconditional, expecting nothing. This causes us to separate the ideas of love and obedience; the best form of love is given irrespective of obedience.

Yet, stop again and think about what the Father meant when he said he was "well pleased" with the Son at his baptism. Why would he have been well pleased? The context of Jesus's baptism provides the answer: Jesus did what neither Adam nor Israel did—obey the Father perfectly (Matt. 4:1–11). The Father loves the incarnate Son because the Son perfectly obeys, even to the death. "For this reason the Father loves me, because I lay down my life that I may take it up again" (John 10:17).

After all, Jesus's food is "to do the will" of the Father and "to accomplish his work" (John 4:34; cf. 6:38; Matt. 4:4). He does "nothing of his own accord, but only what he sees the Father doing" (John 5:19; cf. 14:31). He speaks and teaches just as the Father taught him (John 7:17; 8:28; 12:49–50). He has come in the Father's name and authority, not his own (John 5:27, 43; 7:17; 8:28; 12:49; 14:10). And he abides in the

Father's love by obeying the Father: "If you keep my commandments," says Jesus, "you will abide in my love, *just as I have kept my Father's commandments and abide in his love*" (John 15:10). Startling words, these, especially for a generation of evangelicals raised on the idea that unconditional love is the highest form of love. Jesus "abides" or "remains" (NIV) in the Father's love *because* he has kept the Father's commands. Jesus, too, shows his love for the Father by obeying him. "I do as the Father has commanded me, so that the world may know that I love the Father" (John 14:31).

Jesus was the perfect Davidic son promised in the Psalms, who is rewarded for his righteousness. He was anointed above his companions *because* he loved righteousness and hated wickedness (Ps. 45:7; Heb. 1:9; see also Ps. 21:5–7). And he experienced God's favor because of his righteousness: "The Lord dealt with me according to my righteousness" (Ps. 18:20; cf. Pss. 7:8; 26:1; 35:24).

For Jesus the Son, love leads to obedience, and obedience is a sign of love. For God the Father, love depends upon obedience, and obedience is a condition of love.

In other words, God the Father does not love the incarnate Son indiscriminately. He does not love him "just because," much as you or I wouldn't actually love our friends or spouses "just because." There's a reason or condition for the Father's love, and that reason is the Son's obedience. The Father loves Jesus the Son *because of* his righteousness. He is "well pleased" with the Son's obedience and perfection. He is attracted to that.[8]

If the divine Father's love for the incarnate Son was conditional, does that mean the Son could have lost it? That's another version of the age-old theological question, could Jesus have sinned? No, Jesus could not have sinned, because the triune God cannot sin, and Jesus is God the Son in inseparable relation with the Father. Yet we must remember that Jesus's temptations were real and his obedience really matters, as does

8. I am not saying the Father loved the Son in eternity past because of the Son's "obedience." I would maintain, however, that there is a "because of" to the eternal Father's love for the Son in eternity past. It's not indiscriminate or purposeless. There is a reason for it, whether the eternal Son's holiness or righteousness or all the attributes of his nature or *something*. Here, however, we're peering into mysteries beyond our reckoning.

our obedience. The certainty of Jesus's obedience does not minimize the reality and necessity of his obedience for us. And what matters most for us as sinners is that Jesus perfectly and completely met the conditions, so that our salvation is sure and complete.

Here's the takeaway for us: though we don't share one nature with the heavenly Father the way Jesus does, there are lessons to learn by divinely established analogy from their love for each other. We can follow their example. Two human beings cannot "indwell" one another the way the divine Father indwells the eternal Son, but we can "indwell" one another as the divine Father indwells the incarnate Son. Remember, Jesus prayed that we would be one, like he and the Father are one. In fact, he said it three times (John 17:11, 21, 22).

What does that mean? It means our separate natures begin to share the same DNA, so we want the same things. We can share the same faith, the same ambitions, the same character, the same love. We can give ourselves to one another so that Christ might be exalted in and through one another.

Our oneness means we can participate in a shared identity and glory. My glory is yours and yours is mine because both of us share in the glory of Christ, which is the glory of the Father. Our oneness means we can imitate Christ and imitate one another in the way of Christ. Jesus followed the Father. You follow Jesus. I follow you. Through the links in the chain, I eventually learn to walk in the righteousness of the Father.

This is the life that Paul says is "worthy of the gospel." It's one whereby a church shares "one spirit" and "one mind" and "the same love" (Phil. 1:27; 2:2).

God's God-Centered Love

How might we summarize these four lessons with regard to the divine Father and Son? We might say that God's love is fundamentally God-centered. The Father gives his righteousness and glory to the Son and delights in that glory above all. The Son in turn gives his righteousness and glory to the Father and delights in that glory above all. Never does either surrender the demands of their shared holy and righteous character. The DNA of the divine Father *is* the DNA of the divine Son, which *becomes* the DNA of the human nature of the incarnate Son (see Heb. 5:8). The Father beholds himself in the Son, who is his own image. And the Son displays all the glory of the Father.

There is a win-win dynamic at the heart of all reality because gift and attraction work together. The Father gives and receives, gives and receives, gives and receives. The incarnate Son receives and gives, receives and gives, receives and gives. Until, finally, giving and receiving merge, and authority and obedience merge, like two sides of a coin.

To be sure, there remains an asymmetry between divine Father and incarnate Son in terms of their relations to one another.[9] The Father sends, while the Son goes. The Father commands, while the Son obeys. The Father initiates, while the Son responds. Never on the pages of the New Testament is the order reversed.[10] Still, there are no losers amid these different roles or vocations. The relationship of authority and obedience is no threat to pleasure, glory, and love. Both Father and Son "win" and share in the glory of redemptive victory. Authority and obedience are the vehicle through which love is demonstrated. God the Father gives all he has to Jesus the Son for the Son's eternal joy. The Son, radiating with the Father's own righteousness and glory, gives all he has to the Father for the Father's eternal joy.

It is the archetypal boomerang of love.

Hear Paul: "God has put all things in subjection under his feet," he says of Christ. "When all things are subjected to him, then the Son himself will also be subjected to him who put all things in subjection under him, that God may be all in all" (1 Cor. 15:27–28). Out and back the boomerang whirls.

Conclusion

Much of this chapter may have seemed abstract. But it's the biblical and theological engine that I hope will help you to start rethinking your views of love, at least if your views have been overly formed by the world

9. On the obedience of the "sent Son," see Scott Swain and Michael Allen, "The Obedience of the Eternal Son," *The International Journal of Systematic Theology* 15, no. 2 (April 2013): 114–34.

10. Carson writes, "Not once is there any hint that the Son commissions the Father, who obeys. Not once is there a hint that the Father submits to the Son or is dependent upon him for his own words and deeds" (*Difficult Doctrine*, 40).

we live in. Even the way Christians often talk about love can have a distorting effect.

It's tempting to impatiently say, what difference does this make for me? That's a fine question. But just stop and consider: we've been staring at the very heart and center and source of all the universe—the divine Father's love for the Son. In a sense, there is nothing more important than this. This is the one big story that you cannot miss, because everything in the universe and beyond has its source here.

We'll meditate on these things more concretely in the next chapter. Yet what we've seen so far about God's love is that it's God-centered. The Father gives all he has to the incarnate Son, and he's attracted to and affirms what he sees in the incarnate Son, namely, the Son's obedience. There is no separation of love and obedience.

God's love isn't the kind of gift through which he dissolves into nothingness, like a Buddhist idea of making yourself one with the universe by completely denying yourself. Rather, at the risk of too simple an analogy, I can't help but think that the Father beholds the Son just a tiny bit like how my four-year old looks at a massive ice cream cone and says, "I *love* ice cream!" She takes tremendous pleasure in that cone, and you can imagine the wide eyes and the big smile. The Father, too, takes tremendous pleasure as he beholds the Son, more than he takes in anything else. And so the Son with the Father, the Spirit with both, and both with the Spirit.

This is the white-hot sun at the center of the universe. Isn't that worth marveling at for a while?

4

God's Love for God—Part 2

This chapter is an extension of the last one. The goal here is to unpack and meditate upon what we considered there, particularly since much of the discussion was pretty abstract. Let me try to be more concrete and draw out a few lessons mentioned there.

Remember when you were nine or ten and looked up to your older siblings or their friends? You liked their music, or clothes, or bravado. So you internalized their styles or attitudes. You patterned yourself after them. When I hit adolescence in the mid-'80s, even the supposedly nonconforming punk rockers all copied one another. They all looked the same, with either a skinhead or a Mohawk, a black leather jacket, and Dr. Martens boots. Or, jumping to the 1990s, perhaps you remember how every third woman styled her hair like Jennifer Aniston's in the television show *Friends*.

This is how culture works. We love something and then mimic it. Our sense of self takes shape around our loves. We grow into what we love or, rather, it grows into us. It indwells us, interpenetrates us, refashions us. You are what you love, philosopher James K. A. Smith said in a book by that title.

Here's another example. I spent almost two decades sitting under the preaching of a pastor named Mark Dever, and for the last decade we have worked together. Much of my work involves putting his ideas and instincts, which I love, into words, even while I try to bring my own insights and perspectives to bear. Recently I wrote a book on faith and politics. He read it. And liked it. And humorously quipped how much he recognized it—meaning that he saw many of his own ideas coursing through my pages, both where I had given him a footnote and at a more foundational or DNA level.

Part of me wanted to resist the claim. But I know better. Human natures are imaging, mirror-like, sponge-like things. We absorb and reflect. Very little is original to any of us. I've spent so much time with Mark that his way of thinking, seeing, and responding to the world indwells me, just like my parents and siblings and spouse and friends and so many others indwell me. All of these influences, together with so many technologies and cultural traditions and societal values, like the liturgies of a church, says philosopher Smith, have formed and shaped who I am.

That impulse to resist, however, might explain why I've had difficulty thinking of a classic work of Western literature that presents our social and moral conformity to the world around us in a positive light. Much Western literature pictures the tendency to conform, but such conformity is always cast in a negative light. To grab one of a million examples, think of Henrik Ibsen's play *An Enemy of the People*. For the sake of tourist dollars, a whole town convinces itself to cover up the fact that its natural bath waters are contaminated. One man stands against the crowd and becomes an enemy of the people. The reader, of course, regards him as the hero. Many (perhaps most) Western novels and stories are like this. Through our schooling years, we read, remember, and promote the individual who defines himself over and against the community, whether successfully or not.

I can think of counterexamples, however, when I turn to non-Western or nonwhite literature. In a class on Native American literature in college, the stories centered on a protagonist coming to terms or making peace with the tribe's traditions, rituals, worldview, and gods. Or turning to an African American work, I think of Ta-Nehisi Coates's first book, *The Beautiful Struggle*, an autobiographical work about his childhood and adolescence. It chronicles his attempt to come to terms with what it means to be African American. As a child, he little appreciates his father's hobby of publishing arcane and out-of-print black literature, or his father's history with the Black Panthers. Growing older he reacts to gangsta rap and often feels like the odd-man-out on the streets of Baltimore. Yet at some point he discovers the djembe, an African drum, and takes to it almost as an act of worship. He learns about the history of Africa. Eventually Coates makes his own journey to the Mecca of African American life, Howard University. By the story's end, Coates remains his own man, and he effectively acknowledges that African American identity is a challenged one. But the very challenges give it character and make it weighty, and so Coates inhabits that identity. Or it inhabits him.

Author Miroslav Volf, too, offers a personal picture of how culture indwells us. He does it, in all places, in the acknowledgments of one of his books.

> It seems obvious to say that *I* wrote this book. Mine are its ideas, its organization, its formulations. But that's a superficial kind of "mineness." Most of what's in the book has been given to me. . . . I was able to write this book because I've received from teachers, family, friends, students, and audiences. And I've received in such ways that I often can't tell where what's originally mine stops and where what came from others begins.[1]

We know we're indwelled by others when we don't know where our thinking begins and theirs ends.

It's true that two people cannot indwell one another the way divine Father and divine Son do. The Father and the Son share one nature and essence. Yet, remember we are imaging creatures. That makes an analogy possible. Two people experience something vaguely *like* the Trinity's own mutual indwelling as those people grow in one mind, one spirit, one faith, one love (see Phil. 1:27; 2:2). Christians experience this most profoundly through the gospel, which is why Jesus prays that his disciples "may all be one, just as you, Father, are in me, and I in you" (John 17:21). Yet the backdrop, or the building blocks, of what he prays for the disciples is something common to humanity as imaging creatures. What Volf describes is very human.

1. Miroslav Volf, *Free of Charge: Giving and Forgiving in a Culture Stripped of Grace* (Grand Rapids, MI: Zondervan, 2005), 237.

We have all experienced this with the various groups we have been a part of. I could ask about the crowd you ran with in high school. Did you hang out with the athletes? The cool kids? The theater crowd? The computer squad? Whichever it was, you probably began to think and laugh and lament like your friends did.

In particularly close relationships, as with a husband and wife, we complete one another's sentences. What the gospel and the Holy Spirit do is turn these imaging realities in a Godward direction.

Love and Law

A crucial part of the dynamic at play here is the relationship between love and law. In general, to love something is to internalize its laws, codes, operating principles, or character. Once the law of what you love has been internalized, you radiate with it. You talk about it. You advertise it, both in word and in lifestyle. That's true whether we're speaking about the love of God or the love of a convertible.

Psalm 1 teaches just this. The blessed man of this psalm delights in the law of the Lord, meditating on it day and night. He imbibes and absorbs God's law. Then he glows with it. God's character becomes his character, and as such he becomes like a tree planted by streams of water, yielding its fruit in season, its leaf never withering.

Think once again of Jesus saying, "I do as the Father has commanded me, so that the world may know that I love the Father" (John 14:31). Jesus, the God-man, completely and exhaustively "internalized" God's law, which is an expression of God's character. He did this because he loved the Father more than anything else, and he wanted the world to know the Father even as he knew the Father. The codes and culture and character of heaven indwelled Jesus entirely, making him a purveyor of heaven's principles and postures.

Loving God, then, means internalizing God's law: "This is the love of God, that we keep his commandments" (1 John 5:3). It means internalizing Christ's teaching: "If anyone loves me, he will keep my word" (John 14:23).

Apart from God's Spirit, of course, God's law does not have the power to change us. Yet, by God's Spirit, loving God means loving his law, since it expresses his character. And such love, by the power of God's Spirit, becomes generative in our lives. We grow and expand and become larger as we begin to mimic God. We internalize God's way of being, God's nature, God's rule, his character. As such, we then become like that fruitful tree, blessing those around us.

Consider then all that the doctrine of the Son's incarnation offers us. You and I possess defiled and devastated versions of human nature. But Christ took on our nature. He filled it out, purified it, perfected it. And how beautiful and glorious that nature becomes when he puts it on.

> Fairest Lord Jesus, Ruler of all nature,
> O Thou of God and man the Son,
> Thee will I cherish, Thee will I honor,
> Thou, my soul's glory, joy and crown.
>
> Fair is the sunshine, fairer still the moonlight,
> And all the twinkling starry host;
> Jesus shines brighter, Jesus shines purer
> Than all the angels heaven can boast.

Now, imagine: by the Spirit of Christ we can be conformed to that same image and glory (2 Cor. 3:18; 1 John 3:1–3). One feels nervous to say it. It almost sounds blasphemous. Yet, indeed, Peter promised that we can "become partakers of the divine nature" (2 Peter 1:4). And so Jesus prayed, "The glory that you have given me I have given to them, that they may be one even as we are one, I in them and you in me, that they may become perfectly one, so that the world may know that you sent me and loved them even as you loved me" (John 17:22–23). Notice that in all of this, Jesus is not worried that if the Father begins to love us, there will be less of the Father's love for him. He knows that God's love is a win-win proposition.

Black Hole or Expanding Universe

Let's think a bit further about the life-creating and win-win nature of God's love, with the help of another image. The fallen human being and his or her loves are like a black hole. God's love, however, is like an expanding universe.

I remember a junior high science teacher telling our class that, were an astronaut to sit somehow on the surface of a black hole and try to signal his spaceship with a flashlight, the black hole would suck the light of the flashlight back into itself. That's pretty powerful. Likewise, the fallen human being will suck the entire universe into him- or herself for the celebration of his or her own glory. The self is its own greatest love. It's true that, by God's common grace, even the worst of sinners love their children and friends and spouses. But apart from the restraints of God's grace, they and we will ultimately exploit those we love for our own gain. We will suck them in, even as Eve sucked in Adam and Cain sucked in Abel. Augustine described the sinful nature as a soul curving in on itself.

This universe of self-love is the one I described in chapter 2 as collapsing in on itself. It's like a black hole that shrinks itself into a smaller and smaller space. It's selfish, self-consumed, self-obsessed. It's about me, me, me.

Selfish love always looks like gain, but it always yields loss.

Truly loving another person means forgetting yourself long enough to pay attention to his or her section of the universe. Look at that planet! Look at that solar system! There's always self-sacrifice at the beginning of love: you have to stop thinking about your own planetary system long enough to take notice of the other person's. But as you do, your universe grows; it's like discovering another star you hadn't seen before. So even if a God-like love starts with sacrifice, it's eventually life-creating. It makes things bigger and bigger. I learn to love one friend, then two, then seven, then seventeen. Each friend teaches me, enriches me, expands me. Is that a whole galaxy over there?

A single friend recently told me about his reluctance to have children in light of all the sacrifice that's required. I understood completely. Who enjoys hearing a baby crying at 3:00 a.m.? And helping the kids with piano or with getting to softball practice sometimes means saying no to promising work opportunities. Yet here's what I explained to my friend. Staring at a sacrifice never seems appetizing at first. You don't want to swallow it. But once you do swallow it for the sake of love, you discover that you as a person are nourished and stronger. It's like reaching the top of a rugged hill, looking over to the other side, and discovering an expansive green valley for building a home and planting crops. So, no, I don't like waking up at 3:00 a.m. or saying no to opportunities at work. But I'm no longer the single man I once was. The value of my children and watching their personalities blossom and grow offers a much profounder joy than a night of sleep or a work opportunity. My heart weighs things differently now. The sacrifices changed me, and there is no regret. Thanks to my four daughters, I live in a much bigger universe than the single version of myself ever imagined.

God's love has an outward push and an other-centeredness. This is the first "win" in the win-win of his love. Ironically, though, the outward push and other-centeredness of God's love is a property of his triune nature and an inward push between his own persons. That's the second "win." The outward depends upon the inward. God's mission proceeds from his procession, an older generation of theologians said. By contrast, the monistic (non-triune) God of Islam, by nature, need not love. The Qur'an calls Allah "all-loving" (85:14) and points to creation as evidence of his love. But this is just the Qur'an stealing labels from the Bible.

Consider the backstory of a monistic God like Allah. Before creating a universe, there is no other person for such a God to love. There is just Allah alone, not loving any other person and unloved by any other person. Any love he has is only *inward*. There is no intrinsic *outwardness* to it. Not so with Father, Son, and Spirit in eternity past. God's tri-unity "forces" each person "outward" to the others as they indwell one another in eternal delight and love and joy. And though we must not say that God was constrained to create a universe in order to share his love and glory with still more people, it makes sense that he would. It's suited to his triune nature and the generous nature of his love. We might even say the Father created the universe as a gift to the Son, the Son as a gift to the Father, and both for and from the Spirit.

So again, the outward push of God's love beyond himself to the universe and humanity depends upon the inward push of his love as shared between the three persons. God's other-centered love, within the context of the Trinity, is a kind of self-love. It is utterly God-centered. It is utterly constrained by his law or the requirements of his nature, and it always careens toward the exaltation of his glory, since his glory is the most satisfying and joy-producing thing of all. Yet the inward yields an outward. And that's the boomerang or the win-win. The Father delights in the righteous character of the Son, and the Son in the Father. It's not a relativistic free-for-all. God doesn't most love one thing one day, internalizing it, and another thing another day, internalizing that. He doesn't absorb the fallen cultures of the different cities he inhabits, like we do. His love remains resolutely ordered and pure, resolutely fixed on the best thing—himself. And yet being fixed on himself involves an other-centeredness within himself, which in turn yields his decision to love beyond himself.

God's love produces not a black hole but a universe exploding outward, growing ever larger and larger. Yet that outward explosion works by God's own law, just as the physical universe expands according to the laws of physics. Without physics, the universe collapses on itself.

As such, we will discover in the coming chapters that God's love requires both salvation and judgment. It will prove gracious and discriminating. It embraces and draws lines, all according to the requirements of his character.

The Win-Win Dynamic of God's Love and Glory

It's hard to get our finite and fallen minds around the win-win dynamic of God's love and glory, especially its inward push toward God's self-exaltation. Movie actor Brad Pitt, explaining why he abandoned the Christianity of his youth, spoke for fallen humanity when he said: "I didn't understand this idea of a God who says, 'You have to acknowledge me. You have to say that I'm the best, and then I'll give you eternal happiness. If you won't, then you don't get it!' It seemed to be about ego. I can't see God operating from ego, so it made no sense to me."[2] Pitt's words make intuitive sense. Human glory, as we experience it, is so often

2. Brad Pitt, "I Have Faith in My Family," interview by Dotson Radar, *Parade*, October 7, 2007, http://www.parade.com/articles/editions/2007/edition_10-07-2007/Brad_Pitt.

a zero-sum-game proposition. The glory one team receives by winning the championship game depends upon another team losing. It's how the system works.

Yet there are at least three problems with Pitt's line of thinking. First, he places God and humanity in equivalent moral positions, as if God and humans were entitled to the same things—worthy (or not) of the same things. And if my life shouldn't be "about ego," neither should God's. This assumption fails to recognize that God is not one of us!

Second, God is triune, which means "self" love necessarily involves more than one person. Giving and receiving are merged.

Third, human glory is finite and uncreative, while God's glory is infinite and creative. Pastor John Piper has likened human glory to a leaky bucket of water, and divine glory to a wellspring of water. One quickly runs out. The other offers an unlimited supply of life. It's an excellent illustration. My glory means your loss, but God's glory means your gain, if you belong to God. That's the win-win.

As with God's glory, so with his God-centered love. When God the Father loves God the Son for God's sake, the whole universe gains. Indeed, the universe gets created in the first place! Do you see the life-creating power of God's God-centered love? When you or I love our children ultimately for our own sake or even for their sakes, the universe begins to shrink around us and them. Loving them ultimately for our own sake means exploiting them. Loving them for their sake means spoiling them. In both cases, things get ugly, and we're back to the black hole. Therefore, we must love our children, like God, for God's sake.

True love, Augustine put it so well, is always with respect to God. Any love for spouse or children, friend or neighbor, house or work, that is not given with respect to God is not true love.

Loving God—and loving others with respect to God—then, requires Spirit-empowered obedience. It requires us to internalize God's law, God's culture, God's way of being, as Jesus did. It requires divine mimicry. This is what it means to participate in the divine nature—obediently living and loving like God for the sake of God. This is how we open ourselves up to an infinite universe of divine beauty, while closing ourselves off to the black hole of sin and death. And what else shall

God's people do throughout eternity, but discover the vaster and farther reaches of God's wisdom, love, and righteousness?

In fact, here's what the Serpent in the garden never wanted us to see: to obey God is to share in his rule. Walking in God's ways, for Adam and Eve, meant ruling over the earth with a crown of glory (see Psalm 8). By submitting to the heavenly Father, Jesus, ironically, assumed the authority of the Father. "To be *in* authority," theologian Oliver O'Donovan has remarked, "you have to be *under* it, and if you are under it you are in it."[3]

How different from the love we find on today's movie screens and in university classrooms. Love, says the world, is utterly free, constrained by nothing. Yet love apart from God's law is like an expanding universe trying to ignore the laws of physics. It is like an adulterous free-for-all. You love one thing, then another, then another, until everything is cheapened and sucked dry. In your trail are the charred remains of once-precious lives, while your own universe has contracted and shriveled, like a vacuum in space with all inside and no outside.

Love and Holiness, Inseparable

The world certainly pits holiness and love against one another, just as it pits love and law against one another. Yet so do Christians. For instance, we might retell church history characterizing certain churches or movements as veering too far toward holiness and separation, thereby forsaking love, or veering too far toward love and assimilation, thereby forsaking holiness. The Puritans and the fundamentalists provide common stereotypes for the former overemphasis. The Romantics and the liberals provide common stereotypes for the latter.

But the problem is not putting too much emphasis on one side, as if that required a de-emphasis of the other. The problem is de-emphasizing either. If a church abandons holiness, it abandons love, and if it abandons love, it abandons holiness. God's love and holiness are inseparable.

What is holiness? In some respects, it's the very Godness of God. The seraphim chant,

3. Oliver O'Donovan, *The Desire of the Nations: Rediscovering the Roots of Political Theology* (Cambridge: Cambridge University Press, 1996), 90.

Holy, holy, holy is the Lord of hosts;
the whole earth is full of his glory! (Isa. 6:3)

The Hebrew language will sometimes state a word twice to give it emphasis, as in "gold gold" for really pure gold. But here the seraphim pull out all the stops and say the word three times, as if walking around God in triangular fashion and seeing holiness from every angle. Holiness is what makes God God. It's what sets him apart from everything he has created. In a sense, only he can have it.

In a derivative sense, God's holiness is God's consecration to his glory, which is an attribute we can share. People often define holiness as a separation *from sin,* but it's more than that. It's also consecration *to* something—*to his glory*. The whole earth is full of his glory, the seraphim explain after declaring him holy. The holiness of God does not separate him from the earth. It does just the opposite. It fills the earth with his presence so that he might display his unique and exclusive glory.[4] Showing his glory is showing his holiness, says Ezekiel (28:22; see also Ex. 15:11). Holiness, like love, has both an outward impulse and an inward God-directed impulse. It's not just love that sends missionaries. Holiness does, too. It wants the whole world consecrated to God in worship. So David sings,

Ascribe to the Lord the glory due his name;
worship the Lord in the splendor of holiness. (Ps. 29:2)

What's the relationship between holiness and love? For starters, we might say that God's love is directed by God's holiness. It's constrained by his holiness, as water is constrained by the pipe through which it flows. God's love always and only moves toward holy ends.

More profoundly, we might say that God's holiness simply *is* the love shared between his three persons. That's how Jonathan Edwards describes it: "The holiness of God consist[s] in his love, especially in the perfect and intimate union and love there is between the Father and Son."[5] The Father's love of the Son, for instance, is his consecration to the Son.

---

4. Cf. J. Alec Motyer, *The Prophecy of Isaiah: An Introduction and Commentary* (Downers Grove, IL: InterVarsity Press, 1993), 77.

5. Jonathan Edwards, "Treatise on Grace," in *The Works of Jonathan Edwards*, vol. 21, *Writings on the Trinity, Grace, and Faith*, ed. Sang Hyun Lee (New Haven, CT: Yale University Press, 2003), 186.

In general, we can connect holiness and love by saying that holiness is the measure of love's devotion to God, or the purity of love's devotion to God. How purely does God love God? That's how holy God is. How purely does a man love God? That's how holy a man is.

And God's love is always holy, in both what it gives and why it gives. The Father doesn't give us his love indiscriminately or because he is attracted to something lovely in us. Everything we have is from him (1 Cor. 4:7). He loves us for the sake of his Son. He wants the world to delight in the Son as he does, to say,

> One thing have I asked of the Lord,
>   that will I seek after:
> that I may dwell in the house of the Lord
>   all the days of my life,
> to gaze upon the beauty of the Lord. (Ps. 27:4)

God's holy love, to use the metaphor once more, is a boomerang, swirling outward and drawing us into its arc. For from him, through him, and to him are all things. To him be the glory (Rom. 11:36).

Holy love divides the universe in two. And there's a bright and clear boundary line between the two sides, one as clear as the boundary between the inside of the garden of Eden and the outside, the inside of Noah's ark and the outside, the inside of a house covered by a smear of blood on the night of the Passover and the outside, the inside of the Israelite camp in the wilderness and the outside, the inside of the Promised Land and the outside. It's a boundary as clear as the Jordan River. On one side of the line is *the holy*; on the other side is *the unholy*. On one side are to be those who bear a God-centered love; on the other side are those who love idols. On one side are those who listen to God's Word and God's law; on the other side are those who listen to other voices (see Gen. 3:17).

Summary

What's the takeaway from this chapter and the last one? For starters, we observe that love involves both an affirming or affection for another and giving oneself to the other for the purposes of exalting the other. If it's a holy love, Jesus will always be the one whom we seek to exalt, even as we love another.

God's love itself is God-centered. It is holy. And this holiness is the "condition" or "law" of all God's love. Yet don't misunderstand. Because God is triune, God's love of *self*, mysteriously, involves love of *other*. One God, three persons. The Father beholds his own image in the Son, and so loving the glory and righteousness of the Son is loving himself. God's love goes out and comes back, goes out and comes back, like a boomerang.

We are not triune, which means that love of self and love of others do not merge in the same way. Yet we are created in God's image, which means we must love ourselves and others only with respect to God. All *our* loves, too, must be God-centered. This is the "condition" or "law" for all our loves.

Along the way, we also considered the fact that love and law are not opposites. God's love, like every form of love, both healthy and unhealthy, comes with a set of requirements. This is why Jesus so often referred to love and obedience in the same breath. Love leads to obedience, and obedience is an act of love.

Lest there be any confusion, every form of love, both healthy and unhealthy, imposes a set of laws. The love of a healthy body yields the laws of the diet. The love of learning yields the requirements of study. The love of a mistress rewrites the laws of marriage in the adulterer's mind. What he formally deemed unacceptable he now tells himself is good and necessary.

Love and law, or love and authority, are inseparable. The only question is, what do you most love? Right love leads to right obedience. Wrong love, to wrong obedience. And the standard of right is always the supremacy of God. God is best.

Conclusion: Lessons for a Church

But remember, the purpose of this book, aside from acquiring a better understanding of love, is to prepare the way to better understand the church. So let's conclude the chapter by thinking about what God's holy love, a love epitomized most fully between the divine Father and Son, means for the church. We too have been declared "holy and beloved" (Col. 3:12). Five lessons follow, four of which connect to the path of a boomerang.

1. *The throw—holy love impels a church to evangelize and do good.* A church characterized by holy love abstains from sin, but it also lives among sinners. It's not *of* but it is *in* the world. Holy love sends missionaries around the world and evangelists down the street. It causes Christians to care for the downtrodden, knowing that the downtrodden are created in God's image. It makes them continually mindful of how their lives and actions reflect well or poorly on their Savior among outsiders.

2. *The turn—holy love impels a church to mark off members and practice church discipline.* A church that chooses to emphasize God's love but not God's holiness is a church that doesn't actually understand what God's love is. God's love, I've observed, is wholly fixed upon God and his glorious character in all its aspects. It's holy. A church characterized by holy love, likewise, is jealous for God's glory and fame. Therefore, it seeks to name everyone with whom God has identified himself. Those with whom he identifies himself are, by definition, holy. In the Old Testament, Israel was holy because he declared, "I will be their God, and they will be my people." In the New, Christians are declared holy. We are saved by grace through faith in the work of Christ, but he publicly identifies with us through our baptism and our church gatherings (Matt. 18:20; 28:19).

Meanwhile, churches should also practice church discipline when a member's unrepentant sin—sin the person refuses to let go of—suggests he or she doesn't belong to God. Jesus says to treat the unrepentant person "as a Gentile and a tax collector" (Matt. 18:17). Paul says to "deliver this man to Satan" (1 Cor. 5:5). In other words, stop publicly affirming the person as a believer. Membership and discipline, signified and sealed through baptism and the Lord's Supper, are actions of holy love—love for God, for the church, and for the nations. A church that calls itself loving yet hesitates to draw clear membership boundaries or to practice church discipline has been duped into a man-centered caricature of love. As a worst-case scenario, it may be worshiping an idol.

3. *The return—holy love impels a church to teach and disciple.* Holy love wants to be like God. It desires the path of obedience, divine mimicry, the internalization of heaven's culture. Therefore, it gives itself over to studying God's Word and learning everything Jesus commanded. A church characterized by holy love centers its gatherings on the preaching of God's Word. When the church scatters, the members continue to work to build up one another in the faith.

4. *The catch—holy love motivates a church to worship.* Worship is the goal of all a healthy church's activities, whether gathered or scattered. Such a church prizes God above all, and so it takes God's Words onto its lips in music and prayer, showing that it assents to God's judgments. Whether eating or drinking, rising up or lying down, working or playing, its members live for God's glory.

5. *The culture—holy love creates a distinct and holy culture.* This last point doesn't fit with the arcing boomerang analogy, but it's important nonetheless. Inside the membership of a church is where all the natural powers of culture should be put to supernatural ends.

Remember how your high school friends influenced you? That's one reason why the Christian's life should be the church member's life. You and I need a friend group, or even more, a family, that influences and shapes us in the ways of holiness and love. There in the church we learn to laugh, weep, walk, and love in the ways of God. If you think you can self-manufacture your own culture apart from the weekly, even daily, influences of other believers, you're profoundly self-deceived. Like a family, we don't get to choose all the members of our church. It's within a church that our universe really has the opportunity to expand as we learn to love young and old, wealthy and poor, one ethnicity and another.

In short, churches characterized by holy love possess both an inward and an outward impulse. They are inward in that they conspire to draw people to the love of God; they are outward in that they want more and more people to know this very love. God's holiness and love in the hearts of God's people are a purifying furnace that burns brighter and brighter with love for the lost—that they might know God, and that he might be magnified in their lives.

5

God's Love for Sinners

"In the beginning, God created the heavens and the earth. . . . And God saw everything that he made, and behold, it was very good" (Gen. 1:1, 31). Thus begins the Bible. And thus God's love for the unfallen world looks somewhat similar to the Father's love for his unfallen Son. Like the Father's love for the Son, God's love for creation began with a word of affirmation. He was pleased with what he saw. He felt affection.

Like the Father's love for the Son, God loved creation with respect to himself. The natural universe displayed his creativity, his beauty, and his order. Humanity perfectly displayed his image. Creation had no beauty or glory to offer independently of him. Every good gift came from above.

Like the Father's love for the Son, God's love for creation was demonstrated through *giving* to creation—giving it existence, life, and breath.

But unlike the Father's love for the Son, God gave *of himself* to creation. He did not give *himself*. The creation remained entirely separate from God. The Creator is not the creature. Nothing in Scripture suggests that he identified himself with it entirely, as he does with the Son. Loving creation with respect to himself, paradoxically, was an act of loving both himself and something distinct from himself.

You have probably experienced the same paradox. Perhaps you have built a bird house, or taken a photo, or written a line of poetry or computer code, and then admired it with a measure of joy. That joy can turn into a sinful pride, no doubt, yet that joy can also be righteous: "Look what God has given me the ability to do; he gave me the strength and creativity to do it! Praise him!"

So it is when we behold our own newborn children, as I described at the beginning of chapter 3. The word *selfless,* I said, is not big enough to capture what happens in your heart. Yes, you would give anything for her, but you love her particularly because she is *yours*. She is an extension of you. She bears your image and likeness.

Yet, think about that little girl growing up, doing what the divine Son never did. She sins. And then she sins again, and again, and again. Like father, like daughter, indeed. Sin changes the conversation about love. It presents an obstacle to love because it threatens, sometimes ends, the relationship. Yet here's the remarkable thing we will discover in this chapter as we move from creation to new creation: though God only gave *of himself* in creation, it appears that—dare we say it?—he gives *himself* to us in the new creation.

But first we must start with sin.

My Son, My Son!

If you haven't read Alan Paton's South African novel *Cry, the Beloved Country,* you should. I read it in high school and then picked it up recently, reread a few key chapters, and found myself tearing up within minutes.

The 1948 book worked to expose some of the injustices of South Africa's system of apartheid. Along the way it wrestled with the tension between justice and forgiveness, and how Christians have struggled to hold these two things together.

The action centers on Stephen Kumalo, an aging, black Anglican priest who travels from his rural town to the capital city of Johannesburg. He is searching for his wayward son, Absalom. Perhaps you remember that name. Absalom was the son of King David who betrayed his father, the son for whom David wept, "O Absalom, my son, my son!" (2 Sam. 18:33; 19:4). Absalom Kumalo, too, has abandoned his father for a life that betrays his upbringing. Kumalo's heart, like David's, is rent in two by his son's profligacy, but he still loves his son.

Few things offer as much joy as beholding one's newborn child, and few things cause as much grief as watching that child grow up and turn wayward.

From neighborhood to neighborhood and house to house, Kumalo searches for his son, following one tip after another. Eventually, Kumalo learns that his son has murdered a white man in a bungled robbery attempt. Kumalo finally finds Absalom in jail awaiting trial.

> "My child, my child."
>
> "Yes, my father."
>
> "At last I have found you."
>
> "Yes, my father."
>
> "And it is too late."
>
> To this the boy makes no answer. As though he may find some hope in this silence, the father presses him. "Is it not too late?" he asks. But there is no answer . . .
>
> "I have searched in every place for you."
>
> To that also no answer. The old man loosens his hands, and his son's hand slips from them lifelessly. There is a barrier here, a wall, something that cuts off one from the other.

The main question that plagues the father is why.

> "Why did you do this terrible thing, my child?"
>
> . . . There is a moisture in the boy's eyes, he turns his head from side to side, and makes no answer.
>
> "Answer me, my child."
>
> "I do not know," he says.

The conversation stumbles forward for several more minutes, the father never moving beyond bewilderment, the son mired in shame. Eventually the why question returns.

> "Answer me one thing, my child. Will you answer me?"
>
> "I can answer, father."
>
> "You wrote nothing, sent no message. You went with bad companions. You stole and broke in and—yes, you did these things. But why?"
>
> The boy seizes upon the word that is given him. "It was bad companions," he said.
>
> "I need not tell you that is no answer," said Kumalo. But he knows he will get no other this way. "Yes, I see," he said, "bad companions.

Yes, I understand. But for you, yourself, what made you yourself do it?" How they torture one another. And the boy, tortured, shows again a sign of life.

"It was the devil," he said.

"Oh boy, can you not say you fought the devil, wrestled with the devil, struggled with him night and day, till the sweat poured from you and no strength was left? Can you not say that you wept for your sins, and vowed to make amends, and stood upright, and stumbled, and fell again? It would be some comfort for this tortured man, who asks you, desperately, why did you not struggle against him?"

And the boy looks down at his feet again, and says, "I do not know."

The old man is exhausted, the boy is exhausted, and the time is nearly over.[1]

We can empathize with both father and son. We have experienced shock at someone else's sin: "How could you have done this?" Yet we have also found ourselves unable to explain our own sin: "I don't know how I could have done that." As the prophet said,

The heart is deceitful above all things,
 and desperately sick;
 who can understand it? (Jer. 17:9)

Cry, the Beloved Country doesn't offer simplistic answers: bad companions are to blame; the Devil is to blame; the racist policies of the South African government are to blame. The young man is to blame. There is no denying it.

Absalom's judge is sympathetic to the extenuating circumstances surrounding the young man's crime, but the larger racial controversies roiling the nation make the decision to hang him inevitable. Kumalo spends the night before his son's execution on a mountaintop, praying and meditating on his son: "Would he be awake, would he be able to sleep, this night before the morning? He cried out, 'My son, my son, my son.'"

1. Alan Paton, *Cry, the Beloved Country* (New York: Scribner, 1948), 89–91. Paton did not use quotation marks. I have inserted them for ease of reading.

Love in a Jail Cell

It's commonly observed that we can understand the gravity of sin only when it's held up to the light of God's glory. That's true and primary. Yet it's also worth holding it up to the light of human glory. God crowned us with glory in creation, after all (Ps. 8:5).

So consider how precious the fabric and fire of the soul, so mysteriously intertwined with the organic machinery of the body. How tender every bond of love between two people by which heart and mind merge. How exquisite our enterprises, from the atomic to the cosmic, from cantatas to supercomputers.

No praise to you or me. Praise to the One whose breath animates our every second, and whose image is the source of all things good and beautiful within us.

The tragedy and shame of sin, then, is the tragedy of a soul scorned, a body abused, a garden neglected, a house trashed, a relationship exploited, a civilization corrupted, a world bombed and turned to ash. It is most profoundly the tragedy of Righteousness, Love, and Beauty Himself belittled and blasphemed.

So it is one thing to meditate upon God's love for his perfect Son, as we did in the last chapter. It is another thing to mediate upon God's love for a wayward people like us, who scorn, abuse, neglect, trash, exploit, corrupt, bomb, belittle, and blaspheme. How exactly does love work in a jail cell, where an abandoned father looks with broken heart upon the treacherous son? How does it work in the red-light district, or drug rehab center, or shantytown, or gated community, or large house built on the exploitation of others?

This brings us to the Bible's story of salvation. Son Adam went wayward, as did son Israel, as did son David. As did every daughter: Eve misled Adam. Tamar seduced her father-in-law. Rahab turned to prostitution. Yet in each case, God loved. He reached out to save. He covered shame-faced Adam and Eve in animal skins. He rescued Israel from Egypt and then exile. He preserved David's line. And each of these women, somehow, ended up in the family tree of Christ.

That's the concern of this chapter. How should we understand love's impulse to move outward and embrace the sinner? In particular, how do we understand this outward movement *in light of the God-centeredness, conditionality, and holiness of God's love,* as we considered in the last two chapters? Does he see something beautiful in us that he doesn't have but needs? Does he forsake his holiness and love sinners "just because" or "unconditionally" or "no matter what"?

The arc of the boomerang's sweep includes not only a perfect divine Son but also sinners. Yet how? Answering that requires us to pay attention to another metaphor in the Bible important for understanding love—the metaphor of marriage. God loves his people as a husband does a wife.

Love in Marriage and Sex

Think back to our discussion of Kierkegaard in chapter 2 (p. 49). He distinguished Christian love from romantic love, saying that the romantic focuses on "the favorite's name . . . in distinction from the rest of the world." It "strains in the direction of the one and only beloved" and "is determined by the quality, the beauty and worth, of its object." You see a beautiful woman and you desire her, a powerful man and you are attracted to him. Romantic love, Kierkegaard said, is "evoked" and "motivated" by things like beauty and power. Yet Christian love, he continued, isn't like this. It moves toward both "the evil and the good." It is spontaneous and "overflowing unmotivated."[2]

Is that contrast correct?

Certainly, the Bible promotes the unique marital love between a husband and wife. Call it romantic love, if you want. In Song of Solomon, two lovers are enraptured by one another's look, smell, and touch. Each declares the other's love to be better than wine, and their friends encourage them to get drunk on that love (1:2; 4:10; 5:1). He praises her "two fawns" and "mountain of myrrh," which aren't about deer and tree resin (4:5–6). She tells him to partake of her "choicest fruits" and admires his "polished ivory, bedecked with jewels" (4:16; 5:14). She instructs other women not to awaken love at the wrong time because

2. Søren Kierkegaard, *Works of Love*, trans. Howard Hong and Edna Hong (New York: Torchbooks, 1962), 36, 49, 63, 77.

many waters cannot quench love,
    neither can floods drown it. (8:7; see 2:5, 7; 5:8; 8:4).

Years ago, when I was single, my Christian housemates and I threw a Christmas party. I invited a number of non-Christian friends to the party, including one dating couple whom I'll call Mark and Janet. At one point in the evening, I went looking for Mark and Janet and found them in my bedroom, door closed, sitting on my bed and reading my Bible. They appeared slightly embarrassed, as if they had been sneaking a peek at an inappropriate magazine. They giggled, admitted they were reading the Song of Solomon, and exited the room.

No doubt about it, marital love in the Song of Solomon is sensuous. It's not surprising that even two non-Christians might find it titillating. The book says that marital love feels like wine and fire. Looks like ripening figs and blossoming vines. Smells like saffron and frankincense. Coats the tongue like honey and milk. The pleasures and comforts of marital love are powerful, controlling, life altering.

How fitting, then, that God would adopt the image of marital love to describe his saving love for his people! Forget Kierkegaard.

I'm not saying Song of Solomon is an allegory for Christ and the church. I am saying that the book offers the Bible's longest description of marital love, and that marital love is the metaphor God gives to describe his saving love for his people.

In another passage, God says to Israel, "And I will betroth you to me forever. I will betroth you to me in righteousness and in justice, in steadfast love and in mercy. I will betroth you to me in faithfulness. And you shall know the Lord" (Hos. 2:19–20). *Knowing* the Lord isn't head knowledge. It's betrothal.

Paul, too, employs marital love for describing Christ's love for the church: "Husbands, love your wives, as Christ loved the church and gave himself up for her" (Eph. 5:25). Paul then reaches back to the creation of marriage and sexual intercourse itself, and tells us that God created marriage and physical marital intimacy to point to Christ's love for the church: "'Therefore a man shall leave his father and mother and hold fast to his wife, and the two shall become one flesh.' This mystery is profound, and I am saying that it refers to Christ and the church" (Eph. 5:31–32).

The one-flesh physical union of husband and wife, like marriage generally, is not a permanent reality. Marriage and sex are road signs or shadows. The ultimate destination and three-dimensional substance is the love of heaven. Recall Jesus's promise that "in the resurrection [people] neither marry nor are given in marriage" (Matt. 22:30). Why is there no marriage or sex in heaven? Because you don't need the two-dimensional shadow when you have the substance. You don't need the road sign once you've arrived.

It's worth meditating on this truth for just a moment. Think again of all the sensuous language in the Song of Solomon—wine and fire, honey and milk, saffron and myrrh—language that evokes the physical appetites and experiences of two lovers. Think of the power of romantic and sexual attraction generally, as with the mythical Helen, whose face launched a thousand Greek ships. Think of the power that sex asserts over our culture today—all the political battles, the courtroom controversies, the advertising dollars, the fascination with Hollywood. Think of the yearning that single adults often feel for the friendship, intimacy, and companionship of a good marriage. Think of how profoundly a sexual crime impacts the identity of the victim. Think of how much money and time people devote to appearing attractive or to pursuing some type of sexual or romantic pleasure.

Add all these things together and you behold something very, very powerful—personally, socially, politically, economically, even civilizationally. Perhaps judgment day will reveal the role every nation's marital and sexual practices played in its rise and fall. And yet, for as powerful as these realities are, once again, they're mental road signs, bodiless shadows. Christ's full embrace of the church is the substance. Now, what will that be like in the new heavens and earth?

One of the greatest ironies of the postmodern West might be this: that pleasure for which our culture most emphatically rejects God—sex—is the very thing God has given humanity so that we might have an analogy, a category, a language for knowing what the unadulterated enjoyment of him will be like in glory.

Marriage and sex can terminate in heaven because they anticipate the pleasure of heaven and the intimate knowledge of God. They provide a language for understanding union with Christ. D. A. Carson has written, "It is as if the only pleasure and intimacy in this life that comes close to anticipating the pleasure of the church and her Lord being perfectly united on the last day is the sexual union of a good marriage."[3] So, too, writes John Piper, "God created us with sexual passion so that there would be language to describe what it means to cleave to him in love and what it means to turn away from him to others." And again, "God made us powerfully sexual so that he would be more deeply knowable. We were given the power to know each other sexually so that we might have some hint of what it will be like to know Christ supremely."[4]

In the glory of Christ's loving embrace, we discover the culmination of marriage in general and sex in particular.

Sin as Harlotry and Adultery

Of course, there's a flip side to this analogy. The Bible also illustrates our sin as adultery and harlotry. Sin is, after all, unfaithfulness to God.

In Exodus 34 God describes his name as "Jealous" and then warns his people to not whore after Canaan's gods and sacrifice to them (vv. 14–15). In Leviticus 17, he forbids playing the harlot with goat demons (v. 7); and in chapter 20, playing the harlot with the Ammonite god Molech (v. 5).

But Israel's harlotry involved more than worshiping idols. In Numbers 15 God tells Israel to "remember all the commandments of the LORD, to do them, not to follow after your own heart and your own eyes, which you are inclined to whore after" (v. 39). Spiritual adultery begins with the desires of our hearts.

Jumping to the New Testament, John therefore warns against "the desires of the flesh and the desires of the eyes and pride of life" (1 John 2:16), while James charges, "You adulterous people! Do you not know that friendship with the world is enmity with God?" (4:4).

The whoring heart and eyes aren't just those that pursue goat demons or Molech or Baal. The whoring, adulterous heart is the one that

3. D. A. Carson, *Love in Hard Places* (Wheaton, IL: Crossway, 2002), 191.
4. John Piper, "Sex and the Supremacy of Christ: Part One," in *Sex and the Supremacy of Christ*, ed. John Piper and Justin Taylor (Wheaton: IL: Crossway, 2005), 28, 30.

loves the world more than God. It seeks the pleasures and comfort and approval of the world more than God.

The book of Hosea presents the Bible's most extended and in-your-face use of this theme. God tells Hosea to marry a wife who, God says, will prove unfaithful: "Go, take to yourself a wife of whoredom and have children of whoredom" (1:2). And the prophet's wife, Gomer, makes good on God's prediction. She gives her body to other men and their seed. She bears three children, with textual clues suggesting that only the first is Hosea's.[5] Eventually, she leaves altogether (3:1).

Talk about a shocking setup for a story. You cannot help but sympathize with Hosea. What? A wife of whoredom? Really, God? Yet the sexual dynamic of the image, together with the illegitimate children, helps us perceive the shame and tragedy of sin. It taps into that primal human instinct to protect sexual intimacy and childbearing inside a walled garden, an instinct that even the most calloused secular conscience cannot fully eradicate.

But then, with all our sympathies for Hosea provoked, the book turns on us. God says that Gomer's whoredom illustrates Israel's. And Israel, of course, illustrates humanity (see Rom. 3:9–20). Wait a second—we are Gomer? The book hits us from two angles at once: we naturally *sympathize* with Hosea, but must *recognize* we're Gomer.

Absalom's jail cell *is* Gomer's brothel *is* us apart from God.

We were created by God and for God, but we have been unfaithful. Our eyes and hearts have been drawn to other things. We've not sought our delight and pleasure and satisfaction in him. We have sought it in professional success, fantasies of fame or sex, or nice homes. We've sought it in the approval of others.

God's General Love and Particular Love

Remarkably, God still loves sinners. But how?

In chapter 3, I listed the five ways D. A. Carson says the Bible talks about love (p. 62). Two are relevant here. First, it speaks in a few

5. The text explicitly refers to the first child as his (Hos. 1:3). That's not the case with the second and third children (vv. 6, 8). God then describes them as "children of whoredom" (1:2; 2:4), and he says of the third child, "Call his name Not My People, for you are not my people, and I am not your God" (1:9). It's as if Hosea looks down at the newborn and says, "This is not my child."

prominent places about God's salvific love toward the fallen world. "God so loved the world, that he gave his only Son" (John 3:16). He takes no pleasure in the death of the wicked but calls the wicked to turn and live. Like Kumalo in the jail cell, God pleads, "Turn back from your evil ways, for why will you die?" (Ezek. 33:11). There should be no doubt about it: God loves the world, and he loves "the whole world" (1 John 2:2). Perhaps this broad and general love comes closest to what Kierkegaard had in mind as Christian love.

Yet the Bible speaks about God's saving love in another way—as a particular love for his people. And it speaks this way far more often. Think again of Hosea and Gomer: "And the Lord said to [Hosea], 'Go again, love a woman who is loved by another man and is an adulteress, even as the Lord loves the children of Israel, though they turn to other gods'" (Hos. 3:1). Hosea goes and gets her in her sin, as Christ would one day through his work of offering a ransom for sins on the cross: "So I bought her for fifteen shekels of silver and a homer and a lethech of barley" (v. 2). She would now belong exclusively to him: "And I said to her, 'You must dwell as mine for many days. You shall not play the whore, or belong to another man; so will I also be to you'" (v. 3).

So God says to his people, "I will betroth you to me in faithfulness. And you shall know the Lord" (Hos. 2:20).

God's Covenantal and Incorporating Love

Why does God love his people? Does he see something beautiful in them that he doesn't have but needs? No. If that were so, he wouldn't be God. Does he love them "just because" or "unconditionally" or "no matter what"? Again, no.

Instead, the Father sent his Son into the world to win his bride. Jesus came as that Bridegroom, knowing that the Father had given all things into his hands (John 3:29, 35). The Father then set all his love on this bride for the sake of his Son. He is like the dad at a wedding reception, beholding his new daughter-in-law. He hugs her. Calls her daughter. Welcomes her to the family. Jesus observes, "He who loves me will be loved by my Father" (John 14:21). And again, "For the Father himself loves you, because you have loved me" (John 16:27).

God's saving love for us, then, is an incorporating love, a covenantal love. The Father loves the Son, and we are then incorporated into it by marital covenant. "I will betroth you to me forever."

What happens in a marriage? Two become one. Think of Adam in the garden saying of Eve,

> This at last is bone of my bones
> and flesh of my flesh. (Gen. 2:23)

The narrator then observes: "Therefore a man shall leave his father and his mother and hold fast to his wife, and they shall become one flesh. And the man and his wife were both naked and were not ashamed" (Gen. 2:24–25).

"Bone of bone and flesh of flesh" was Adam's way of saying, "This is my flesh and blood—my family." It's like "born again" biology—biology by marital covenant. He leaves the people with whom he shares actual blood and DNA, and becomes a new family with her. Their one-flesh union then symbolizes this one biology, as they literally become one through an indwelling.

In the creation picture, a man and woman are bare. They don't attempt to hide themselves but remain exposed. They take their very identity and make it vulnerable to and dependent on the other person. They let themselves be defined by the other person. Her bone, my bone; her flesh, my flesh. The covenantal bond that unites them is stronger and more profound than blood or DNA, because it is God who joins them together (Matt. 19:6).

Likewise, when does Christianity begin? When we become utterly bare before God by confessing our sin to him. The Father then unites us to his Son through the new covenant of his blood. All the sin that is ours becomes his, and all the riches that are his become ours, like a couple on their wedding day uniting assets and liabilities. Marriage and marital intimacy, we saw a moment ago, are just a dim picture of this.

It's not his bone, my bone; his flesh, my flesh. It's his righteousness, my righteousness; my sin, his sin. Do you see the marital or covenantal exchange?

As part of that exchange, the Father loves us with the love with which he loves the Son. Again, there is an indwelling. The Father is in the Son, the Son is in us, and so the love of the Father for the Son is in us. Jesus says to the Father: "I in them and you in me . . . so that the world may know that you . . . loved them even as you loved me" (John 17:23).

It's remarkable. Like swallowing an ocean.

God the Father gives all the love he has for the Son to us—the beloved Son, the matchless Son, the never-sinned Son, the "fairest Lord Jesus, ruler of all nature" Son, the Son with whom he breathed out and sculpted the universe. He loves the Son with a God-is-love love. And now we are incorporated into this same God-is-love love.

> O the deep, deep love of Jesus,
>   vast, unmeasured, boundless, free!
> Rolling as a mighty ocean
>   in its fullness over me!
> Underneath me, all around me,
>   is the current of Thy love
> Leading onward, leading homeward
>   to Thy glorious rest above![6]

God does not just give *of himself* to us to through Christ. He gives *himself* to us through Christ. We don't become God. But Christ identifies his very self with us (see Matt. 18:20; Acts 9:5), and all the glory that is his becomes ours. Jesus prays, "The glory that you have given me I have given to them, that they may be one even as we are one" (John 17:22). And Paul promises, "For all things are yours, whether Paul or Apollos or Cephas or the world or life or death or the present or the future—all are yours, and you are Christ's, and Christ is God's" (1 Cor. 3:21–23).

And one day, the Bible promises, we will find ourselves sitting at the marriage supper of the Lamb.

More Contra-Conditional Than Unconditional

So is God's love for sinners unconditional? I think the better phrase is contra-conditional. I understand why Christians often refer to God's unconditional love. Salvation through Christ is God's pure gift

6. Samuel Trevor Francis, "O the Deep, Deep Love of Jesus," 1875.

of love to undeserving sinners. We cannot earn it. We receive it apart from anything in us but in shocking contradiction to what we are. And from time to time, for expediency's sake, I refer to God's unconditional love.

Still, we need to keep three things in mind when we do use that term. First, someone had to pay a price in order for God to carry through on his love for sinners, a tab which the bridegroom gratefully picked up. Second, the Bridegroom and his Father require the bride to turn away from other lovers and devote herself entirely to him, apart from which she remains under God's wrath: "Whoever believes in the Son has eternal life; whoever does not obey the Son shall not see life, but the wrath of God remains on him" (John 3:36). Third, those who truly love Jesus *will* obey his commandments: "Whoever has my commandments and keeps them, he it is who loves me" (John 14:21).

Why is it important to keep these three things in mind if we use the language of unconditionality? Remember what I said in chapter 2. Emphasizing only the "pure gift" nature of God's love tempts us toward theological liberalism and ecclesiological pragmatism. Theologically, universalism will make more and more sense. Ecclesiologically, church membership and discipline, which signify the line between the church and world, will make less and less sense.

Better than "unconditional love," I think, is the phrase coined by David Powlison: contra-conditional love.[7] God loves us *contrary* to what we deserve. After all, there are always conditions on God's love, like the three just mentioned. Most fundamentally, his love is always *conditioned* by his holiness. Still, God gives us the gift of his love even though we have lived contrary to his holiness and his law. He loves us, we've been saying, because of his love for the Son and because of the Son's work of righteousness. Our salvation depends on Christ's righteousness, not our own.

Loving us for Christ's sake means that God loves us with a purpose—to conform us to the image of Christ, that the glory of Christ might shine all the more through us.

---

7. See David Powlison, "God's Love: Better Than Unconditional," in *Seeing with New Eyes* (Phillipsburg, NJ: P&R, 2003), 163–70.

> Christ loved the church and gave himself up for her, that he might sanctify her, having cleansed her by the washing of water with the word, so that he might present the church to himself in splendor, without spot or wrinkle or any such thing, that she might be holy and without blemish. (Eph. 5:25–27)

> And we all, with unveiled face, beholding the glory of the Lord, are being transformed into the same image from one degree of glory to another. (2 Cor. 3:18a)

The fire of the Father's affection for the Son is so great that he wants hundreds of millions of faces to look just like Jesus's face. It's ultimately about Jesus.

To tie this section to the last one, we can say that God's contra-conditional love is an incorporating and covenantal love. It depends upon the sovereign Son's vow "I do." Yet that "I do" does not go unanswered, as if Hosea were sitting alone at home mourning his wayward wife. Rather, the Son's "I do" will be joined by our own "I do." God calls, we answer: "I will betroth you to me forever . . . and he [who was Not My People] shall say, 'You are my God'" (Hos. 2:19, 23).

God places his Spirit within our hearts, says Jeremiah, so that we follow and obey willingly. The marital covenant is mutually kept because "God himself makes it so."[8] Repentance and faith, says the New Hampshire Confession, are both "sacred duties" and "inseparable graces." We *do* them, and this doing is a gift of grace. We keep this marital covenant for better, for worse, in sickness and in health. Wonderfully, however, death doesn't part us. The covenant perseveres through death and beyond.

Meanwhile, all the riches of the Father's love for his beloved Son are extended to us. Notice the relationship between John 10 and John 17. Just as Father and Son are one (10:30), so Jesus asks his Father to make

---

8. This phrase comes from Karl Barth, *Church Dogmatics*, IV.1, *The Doctrine of Reconciliation*, ed. G. W. Bromiley and T. F. Torrance, trans. G. W. Bromiley (New York: T&T Clark, 2004), 23. For a more extended discussion on this point, particularly in light of the older conversation about the unilateral versus bilateral nature of God's covenants, see Jonathan Leeman, *Political Church: The Local Assembly as Embassy of Christ's Rule* (Downers Grove, IL: IVP Academic, 2016), 252–54. For an introduction to Barth's approach to the covenants, see Petrus J. Grabe, *New Covenant, New Community: The Significance of Biblical and Patristic Covenant Theology for Contemporary Understanding* (Waynesboro, GA: Paternoster), 194–95, 201–3.

his people one (17:11, 21–23). Just as Jesus has been *consecrated* by the Father (10:36), so he asks the Father to consecrate his disciples (17:17). Just as Jesus says the Father sent him into the world (10:36), so he asks the Father to send his people into the world (17:18, 21, 23). Just as Jesus says that the Father is in him and that he is in the Father (10:38), so he asks his Father, "That they also may be in us. . . . I in them and you in me" (17:21, 23, 26).[9]

In the outward throw of the boomerang of God's love, God's people are incorporated into all the affections, entitlements, and purposes the Father gives to the Son. You can almost picture a wealthy man standing with his son and the son's new bride on their wedding day outside the family mansion. The father points to the mansion, the multicar garage, the antique and sports car collection, the pool and tennis court, the orchards, the vineyards, the garden and sculpted shrubbery, and the crowd of servants rushing around serving wedding guests. He tells his new daughter-in-law that everything she sees belongs to his son, and therefore everything belongs to her. She has done nothing to earn it. Perhaps she has even offended the father through the engagement. Yet now, with a heart overflowing with affection, he gladly gives these riches to her. Why? Because he loves his son.

What Is Love?

Having thought about God's love for God and God's love for sinners, we can systematize the various ways the Bible talks about love.

What is love? Or more to the point, what is true biblical love? *Love is affectionately affirming that which is from God in the beloved, and giving oneself to seeing God exalted in the beloved.* Let me unpack both parts of that definition.

1. *Love is affectionately affirming that which is from God in the beloved.* True love, holy love, always begins here. It is how the divine Father

9. Richard Bauckham makes this connection between John 10 and 17. What Jesus affirms about himself and the Father in chap. 10 he then asks the Father to give us in chap. 17 (Richard Bauckham, "The Holiness of Jesus and His Disciples in the Gospel of John," in *Holiness and Ecclesiology in the New Testament*, ed. Kent E. Brower and Andy Johnson [Grand Rapids, MI: Eerdmans, 2007], 109; cf. A. J. Köstenberger, *The Missions of Jesus and the Disciples according to the Fourth Gospel* [Grand Rapids, MI: Eerdmans, 1998], 186–97).

loved the Son: "this is my beloved Son." It is how God loved his creation: "And God saw that it was good." This is how the lover beholds the beloved in the Song of Solomon. Her beauty is not hers. It's God's. And this is how the parent beholds the child. Mom and Dad look down and see their image, which is the image of God. They see a boy or girl fearfully and wonderfully made.

Love says, "I affirm you. You are worthy and precious and beautiful to me because you are from God."

Affectionately affirming what is from God is the beginning of empathy and compassion. What is compassion? It is love's reaction to seeing one of God's creatures—and especially one of his image bearers—hurting, oppressed, caught in sin, or otherwise under duress. Such love looks upon the slave, the beggar, the neglected child, yet also the person entangled in sin, like Absalom Kumalo; it sees God's image, and it burns with compassion. Such love is drawn to the person who is suffering or caught in sin. It wants to see the bruised reed made strong, the smoldering wick fanned into a flame. It knows to take great caution around sin, but does not forsake loving the person caught in the "big" sins, the strange sins, the more heinous sins (Jude 23; see also Gal. 6:1–2). The greater one's knowledge of God, the greater and better calibrated is one's compassion. There is such a thing as misplaced compassion. Compassion must be given with respect to God and his law, even if one is not consciously thinking of God.

Affectionately affirming that which is from God is also the beginning of righteous indignation toward injustice. Such love beholds the oppressed and is angry at the oppressor, sees the abused and rages at the abuse.

Likewise, affectionately affirming what is from God is the beginning of justification. When you love something, not only do you *want* to justify it; you have *begun* to justify it. Indeed, the Christian doctrine of justification is like love draped in a judge's wig. Where love gives the affirming word "That's valuable and good and worthy," justification enters the courtroom and says, "That's righteous." Love and justification, therefore, typically work in tandem. Both affirm.

An illustration of the connection between love and justification can be seen, ironically, in today's LGBT movement. The movement has nearly succeeded in morally justifying a homosexual identity and lifestyle in the eyes of the broader public, and it has done so in part through the rubric of *love*. "If you love me, you'll accept me as I am." "Don't be a hater." So a son comes home from college, tells his father that he's gay, and insists that loving him means accepting his gay self-identification. At that moment, the father, who no doubt feels a proper compassion for his son and his son's struggle, will be sorely tempted to stretch that compassion to a place it should not go by affirming as righteous something that God calls sin.

Biblical love always begins with the love of God, and therefore it will affirm only what is from God. Sin and folly are never from God. Yet, when God rests lightly on our hearts, we begin to affirm sin and think we are serving both God and love in doing so. The trouble is, sin produces death, and so affirming sin is not love at all, but cowardice and hate.

2. *Love is . . . giving oneself to seeing God exalted in the beloved.* It's no secret that parental "love" can become oppressive. And romantic "love" can become invasive and perverted. "Every breath you take, every move you make . . . I'll be watching you," sang The Police.[10] What keeps such affection from becoming self-serving? Biblical, godly love takes pleasure in the other person's good, and that good is always God. Biblical love therefore gives itself to seeing God exalted in a person's life.

Different occasions call for expressing love differently. Sometimes we share the gospel. Sometimes we do justice. Sometimes we wash the dishes or pick up the kids at school. Sometimes we correct and rebuke. Sometimes we even sacrifice our lives. Yet the point is that such love is always given with respect to Christ. Love's uppermost goal, whether in speaking or acting, is for people to know God in Christ. This is the demand of holy love.

Just as different occasions call for different expressions, so we give ourselves and our love to people in different degrees and ways. To my wife and children one way, to my fellow citizens another way. We give ourselves most completely to family members and, sometimes, close friends. We give *of* ourselves to people further from the center of our lives.

10. Sting, "Every Breath You Take," track 7, on *Synchronicity*, The Police, A&M, 1983.

Yet a Christian always gives himself to Christ entirely. And that means, in every case, biblical love longs to see Christ exalted in another person's life, whether that is our spouse or the person sitting next to us on the airplane. True love always loves with respect to God.

The Joy of Being Loved

One glory of love is that we discover pleasure in doing Godward good for others. This is the point missed by interpreters of Luther such as Kierkegaard, Nygren, and Barth. It's what Augustine, Aquinas, and Edwards understood better. God-centered love involves giving and receiving joy, even if the receiving is sometimes delayed, because God is most joy giving.

For instance, I once worked as a magazine editor. It was around then that I began to grow in the Christian faith, such that my love grew for the men in my Bible study. I recall sitting at my desk at work, distracted from editing, because I wanted to email the men in the study. Encourage them. Check how they were doing. That burgeoning love for these brothers was costly, from the standpoint of my magazine work. Yet it also afforded me a new pleasure—the pleasure of seeing these brothers grow in the grace of God. Eventually, experiences like these prompted me to quit the magazine and turn to vocational ministry.

To be fair, the Augustinian tradition has its weaknesses as well. Specifically, it can underemphasize the fact that God's love, in boomerang fashion, swirls outward and affirms people. The tradition sometimes describes the enjoyment of God as a beatific vision in which we merely sit and behold God—"Like looking at the Grand Canyon," said one preacher. The Bible does include the beatific vision ("to gaze upon the beauty of the Lord"—Ps. 27:4), but it includes more. It illustrates coming into God's presence as a wedding feast, where we share in the embrace and the joy of the Bridegroom. Edwards observes:

> The creation of the world seems to have been especially for this end, that the eternal Son of God might obtain a spouse toward whom he might fully exercise the infinite benevolence of his nature, and to whom he might, as it were, open and pour forth all that immense

> fountain of condescension, love, and grace, that was in his heart, and that in this way God might be glorified.[11]

The affirming nature of God's love for us is indeed precious.

I recall experiencing the joy of such affirmation after I shaded the truth with a fellow elder. He had asked me about my prayer life. I told him that I prayed more than I do. Right after that, I felt deep shame for having lied, but I was too proud to correct the error promptly. By God's grace, I had difficulty sleeping that night, and in the morning I confessed my lie to him. Immediately and graciously, he forgave me. Tears came to my eyes with his forgiveness. In spite of my sin, I was affirmed—remarkably, graciously, wonderfully affirmed. There was no glory to me in that; in fact, there was just the opposite—glory to him who forgave me.

Still, the Augustinian thrust is exactly right. Love is inherently God-centered. Love concerns the praise and worship and glory of God. Love is the enjoying of God and the enjoying of him everywhere he is manifest. So we can scarcely pray better than Paul does when he asks the Father to enable the Ephesians "to know the love of Christ that surpasses knowledge, that [they] may be filled with all the fullness of God" (Eph. 3:19).

Lessons for a Church

What lessons for the church do we gain from this chapter? Several concerning the church's mission stand out.[12] And then a last comment on church covenants is worth mentioning.

1. *Making disciples must be uppermost in the church's mission.* This lesson is an obvious inference from the definition of love provided above. Our uppermost desire for people is that they would know God or know him better. A loving church will therefore give itself centrally to disciple making through evangelism, preaching, and the discipling of its

11. Jonathan Edwards, "The Church's Marriage to Her Sons, and to Her God," in *The Works of Jonathan Edwards*, vol. 25, *Sermons and Discourses 1743–1758*, ed. Wilson H. Kimnach (New Haven, CT: Yale University Press, 2006), 187.

12. For a fuller summary of my views on the mission of the church, see Jonathan Leeman, "Soteriological Mission," in *Four Views of the Church's Mission*, ed. Jason S. Sexton (Grand Rapids, MI: Zondervan, 2017), 17–45.

members. The priority should be reflected in the budget, the pastors' job description, and the conversations of members throughout the week. Pastors should share the gospel in their sermons every week. Members should pursue their non-Christians friends evangelistically, as occasion permits. And congregants should always seek to encourage their fellow members toward greater holiness and love.

The point here is not that we should do good to our friends and neighbors for the sole purpose of turning every conversation into an evangelistic encounter, like a bait and switch. It's just that we love them best when we know their greatest good will be found only in the knowledge of God. Therefore, all our words and deeds will be imbued with that hope.

Within the story of *Cry, the Beloved Country*, Paton mentions those who would criticize this priority. In view of South Africa's racial and economic disparities, unnamed voices disparage one gospel preacher:

> They say he preaches of a world not made by hands, while in the streets about him men suffer and struggle and die. They ask . . . what folly is it that seizes upon so many of their people, making the hungry patient, the suffering content, the dying at peace? And how fools listen to him, silent, enrapt, sighing when he is done, feeding their empty bellies on his empty words.[13]

Paton doesn't answer the critics outright, but he doesn't seem sympathetic with them either. It should be clear to us: there can be no peace and no justice apart from God, whose glory we have offended.

The gospel's work of forgiveness comes first because God is the measure of all things. Sin against others is "sin" only because it's sin against him (Ps. 51:4). Sin means falling short of *his* glory and *his* law, not yours or mine. To treat our sin against God and our sin against others as coequal is to make us—as one false teacher put it—"like God" (Gen. 3:5).

First and foremost, people must be made right with God. For the sake of love, this priority must be clear in every church's mind. Recall Augustine's challenge: "Whoever, therefore, justly loves his neighbor

13. Paton, *Cry, the Beloved Country*, 83–84.

should so act toward him that he also loves God with his whole heart, and his whole soul, and with his whole mind."[14]

2. *Christians should be a people of compassion and justice.*[15] The Great Commission highlights making disciples, but a disciple once made will live like a disciple. He or she will learn to obey everything Jesus has commanded, including all that the Bible says exhorting us to compassion and doing justice.

The gospel's work of forgiveness is uppermost. Yet we cannot separate sin against others from sin against God: "If anyone says, 'I love God,' and hates his brother, he is a liar" (1 John 4:20). Which means that Christians necessarily care about justice. And we cannot separate our faith from a life of obedience: "You see that faith was active along with his works, and faith was completed by his works" (James 2:22). Faith and deeds are inseparable just as loving God and people are inseparable. A church, then, is where we learn to model true justice and compassion for the nations. That justice and compassion should characterize our own life together and then spill outward into the public square.

I'm personally of the conviction that church budgets and pastoral job descriptions should be devoted to *equipping* the saints for doing works of compassion and justice, not so much to *undertaking* those projects on behalf of the saints. You might think of the difference between law schools and lawyers, or medical schools and doctors. The school and the practitioner have slightly different jobs to do, and both are needed. Love requires both equipping and doing.

That said, elders need to be men whose lives model not just good words but also good works. Paul himself was anxious to care for the poor (Gal. 2:10). He exhorted Timothy to watch not just his doctrine but also his life (1 Tim. 4:16). He challenged Titus to be a model of good works and to teach others to do the same (Titus. 2:7, 14; 3:8, 14). And he listed "hospitable" as one of the qualifications of an elder (1 Tim. 3:2).

---

14. Augustine, *On Christian Doctrine*, trans D. W. Robertson, Jr. (New York: Macmillan, 1958), 19 (1.22).

15. For a fuller summary of my views on doing justice, see Jonathan Leeman, "Justice: Not Just Rights, but Right," in *How the Nations Rage: Rethinking Faith and Politics in a Divided Age* (Nashville: Nelson, 2018).

3. *Christians should seek to display God's glory in their lives together and apart.* The mission of the church, in the broadest sense, is to display the image and glory of God. We do this when we gather around his Word, and we do this as we scatter throughout the week to share the gospel, do good, and be good. If God-centered love seeks both to affirm that which is from God and to see God exalted in the lives of others, church members will increasingly view their gathered and scattered lives as opportunities to display God's glory. They will be mindful of their roles as salt and light, and so strive to be distinct. They will love one another as Jesus loved them, and so strive to forgive each other and care for one another's needs (John 13:34–35).

4. *To belong to a church is to belong to a covenant.* A membership covenant is not exactly like a marital covenant. There are different kinds of covenants, after all. You should never break a marital covenant, but Christians should remain free to transfer from one church to another, so long as the process of church discipline has not begun.[16] Yet what makes our relationships in a church covenantal is the fact that Christ has united us to himself through the new covenant of his blood. And Jesus left instructions for us to live out this new covenant locally and publicly. He therefore promised to be present wherever two or three gather in his name. That doesn't mean he will hover as a mystical fog when three Christians enjoy a picnic at the park. It means he will identify himself with our stated assemblies, assemblies that are formally bound together with a kind of legal glue (the courtroom principle behind "two or three") through our shared profession of his name (Matt. 18:20). I am suggesting, in other words, that there is a biblical basis for what we sometimes call church covenants.[17] I don't care if you call it that. The point is, Jesus means for

16. On this point, see Jonathan Leeman, "The Preemptive Resignation—A Get Out of Jail Free Card?," 9Marks (website), February 25, 2010, https://www.9marks.org/article/preemptive-resignation-get-out-jail-free-card/.

17. For my discussion on this point, see Jonathan Leeman, *Understanding the Congregation's Authority* (Nashville: B&H, 2016), 34–36; for a more in-depth treatment, see Leeman, *Don't Fire Your Church Members: The Case for Congregationalism* (Nashville: B&H Academic, 2016), 100–104. See also Patrick Schreiner's helpful discussion of the meaning of Christ's presence in *The Body of Jesus: A Spatial Analysis of the Kingdom in Matthew*, ed. Chris Keith (New York: Bloomsbury T&T Clark, 2016), 147–50.

Christians to take real responsibility for one another's profession of faith and discipleship.

Christians cannot fulfill their new covenant obligations of love and holiness with all Christians everywhere. Just as we could say, "Don't tell me you belong to the army if you never report for duty anywhere," so I'd say, "Don't tell me you belong to the new covenant if you never 'put on' the new covenant with actual brothers and sisters in Christ." We practice, we exercise, we "put on" those obligations to Christ's new covenant people concretely in local churches. The local church is where we have the opportunity to say: "This is my family. I am responsible for them, and they are responsible for me. When one of them is shamed, I am shamed. When one of them is honored, I am honored" (see 1 Cor. 12:26). The church is also the place where we'll be held accountable to our covenantal vows of repentance and faith. If we have not covenanted together with a local church, how do we know we're not self-deceived about our commitments?

When Christians affirm one another's professions of faith through baptism and the Lord's Supper, we effectively make the invisible new covenant visible: "Because there is one bread, we who are many are one body, for we all partake of the one bread" (1 Cor. 10:17).

Conclusion

What does love look like in such a distinct, covenantal society, where we prioritize making disciples narrowly but displaying God's glory broadly? It can look like many things:

- A small group of single young men visiting an elderly widow in the nursing home on Friday night
- A small group of single women inviting an elder's wife to their study to learn from her
- One younger brother in the faith saying to an older brother: "I can't get myself to read my Bible. Can I come to your house every morning and just sit in on your quiet times?"—and doing that for a year and a half
- A white woman, realizing that she harbors racism in her heart, confessing that racism to an African American man and his wife,

and asking for friendship and for help; and that man loving her and helping her

- A group of Asian American college students deciding to join, for the first time in their lives, a non-Asian church
- Crying with a couple after their fourth miscarriage in a row
- Rebuking a man for the way he speaks to his wife
- Rejoicing with a brother when he gets the job promotion that pushes him further than you
- Having neighbors over for dinner several times and having long conversations about the gospel
- Explaining Christianity to the entire fraternity house or football team
- Praying and pursuing work together in a nearby soup kitchen/gospel mission
- Praying and pursuing work together in a nearby crisis pregnancy center
- Leading a church reading group that chooses books relevant to the nation's ongoing race conversation
- Looking for ways to disciple members toward leadership
- Giving thousands annually to care for other members in need
- Looking for ways to help raise one another's children and disciple one another's teenagers
- Thinking all week, "I can't wait to be with the whole family on Sunday."
- Having that awkward conversation where you confess sin and ask for help in the fight
- Regular meals, regular prayers, regular texts and emails and phone calls and "just stopping by"

All these are examples from my own church. Yet, make no mistake, it's a church filled with people who were once Absaloms and Gomers and every other kind of sinner. We are not an assembly of the naturally righteous. We are an assembly of the forgiven.

By God's grace, however, we can see more and more of God's work in one another. And more and more, we give ourselves to seeing Christ exalted in one another's lives. These are the tasks of every church.

6

Love and Judgment

It's a caricature. It confirms the world's worst stereotypes about hypocritical churches and Christian leaders. But William Faulkner's novel *As I Lay Dying* accurately portrays too many ministers and professing Christians who pervert the good news of Christianity.

Addie Bundren, wife and mother in rural Mississippi, is dying. Her children and husband take turns recounting their experiences of watching Mother expire, each coping differently with their shared loss. Then, midway through the story, for three brief pages, Faulkner introduces one more character—the whited sepulchre Reverend Whitfield. No background is provided. Faulkner simply drops the reader into a new subplot with the reverend's own words:

> When they told me she was dying, all that night I wrestled with Satan, and I emerged victorious. I woke to the enormity of my sin; I saw the true light at last, and I fell on my knees and confessed to God and asked His guidance and received it. "Rise," He said; "repair to that home in which you have put a living lie, among those people with whom you have outraged My Word; confess your sin aloud. It is for them, for that deceived husband, to forgive you: not I."[1]

1. This and following quotations are from William Faulkner, *As I Lay Dying* (New York: Vintage International, 1990), 177–79.

Like Hawthorne's Reverend Dimmesdale, Faulkner's Reverend Whitfield once had a secret affair with a member of his flock, Addie. He recalls that "she had sworn then that she would never tell it," but he realizes that "eternity is a fearsome thing to face." So he determines to beat her to the punch.

Traveling by horseback to the Bundren family home, Whitfield prays, "Praise to Thee, O Mighty Lord and King. By this token shall I cleanse my soul and gain again into the fold of Thy undying love." Ah, a true Christian, this Whitfield. The man has sinned and now seeks peace with God and peace with neighbor. He yearns once more for the Lord's love and forgiveness. After praying silently, he says: "I knew then that forgiveness was mine. . . . It was already as though it were done. My soul felt freer, quieter than it had in years; already I seemed to dwell in abiding peace as I rode on. To either side I saw His hand; in my heart I could hear His voice: 'Courage. I am with thee.'"

How fortunate that he feels God's forgiveness before reaching the Bundren home! For she dies before he arrives. The need for a messy confession has passed; God "is merciful; He will accept the will for the deed."

Whitfield then enters the grief-stricken home, reflects on the deceased woman now facing "the awful and irrevocable judgment" for her sin, and pronounces magisterially, "God's grace upon this house." Addie might lie in hell, her sin unconfessed, but Whitfield can rejoice for his own soul's sake: "Praise to Thee in Thy bounteous and omnipotent love; O praise."

After the publication of *As I Lay Dying*, Faulkner was asked in an interview if Whitfield was a hypocrite. He answered: "No, I wouldn't say he was a hypocritical man. He had to live a hypocritical life. That is, he had to live in public the life which the ignorant fanatic people of the isolated and rural South demand of a man of God, when actually he was just a man like any of them."[2]

The caricature well embodies how the world views Christianity, the church, and our talk of love, righteousness, and forgiveness. And there's

2. Frederick L. Gwynn et al., eds., *Faulkner in the University* (Charlottesville, VA: University of Virginia Press, 1959), 114.

merit to the caricature. Scoundrels like Whitfield, a tawdry television preacher before the age of television, do exist. It's not difficult to think of fallen leaders, fallen Christians, or fractured churches that confirm this stereotype.

What's tragic, therefore, is that Whitfield seems to be no Christian. He is a counterfeit, and, like all counterfeits, he makes us cynical and steels us against the real thing. The irony that people often miss is that counterfeits simultaneously hide and reveal something. There is something true in Reverend Whitfield's religion that is beautiful and glorious, even though Faulkner's cartoon drawing contorts it beyond all recognition: there is an all-loving God who exercises his bounteous love in the very act of saving some and not others. There is an all-loving God who displays his gracious love in the very act of forgiving the worst of hypocrites and adulterers. And there is an all-loving God who beckons the praise of a marked-off, set-apart people as he pronounces his blessing upon them and calls them to pronounce that blessing among others: let the nations praise his generous and powerful love.

But who would believe it when hypocrites like Whitfield hit the headlines?

Hypocrisy or heresy will always get more publicity when it involves a church leader like Whitfield, but headlines aren't our main concern. Our own lives are, and the lives of average church members. For every act of hypocrisy that hits the press, are there not ten thousand instances in our own lives, some small and some not so small? Our non-Christian neighbors, colleagues, and friends hear us profess the name of Christ with our mouths and with our church affiliations, yet they watch us and wonder, "If Jesus is all you say he is, why does your life look like mine? Can the gospel you talk about really be true?" More than the headline makers, it's the daily life of the average Christian that ultimately forms the world's perception of Christ and his gospel.

Let Him Be Removed

Paul wrestles with this kind of moral tragedy in 1 Corinthians 5. A man in the Corinthian church was sleeping with his father's wife (probably a stepmother). The apostle exclaims, "It is actually reported that there is sexual immorality among you, and of a kind that is not tolerated even among pagans" (v. 1). Paul had several concerns:

- He was concerned about the name and fame of Christ.
- He was concerned about the church, its witness, its holiness.
- He was concerned about the man, that he was self-deceived and living in danger of damnation.
- He was concerned about holy love—God's, the church's.

Too bad Reverend Whitfield had none of these concerns, and too bad he didn't have a Paul in his life or church.

Paul's solution is straightforward: "Let him who has done this be removed from among you" (v. 2). Paul has "already pronounced judgment" on the man (v. 3). Now he wants the church *not* simply to execute his decision, like a policeman enforcing the decision of the city council. He wants the church to imitate him by entering into the same act of judgment: "Is it not those inside the church whom you are to judge?" (v. 12).

Paul apparently learned from Jesus, who earlier instructed churches to remove members who refused to let go of their sin (Matt. 18:17).

The Boomerang's Return Flight and the Judgments of Love

Both of these stories bring us to the emotionally fraught topic of the relationship between judgment and love. How many times have you heard the phrase "Don't judge me"? And didn't Jesus say something about not judging (see Matt. 7:1)?

Jesus's point was that we should not presume to be anyone's final judge. But our daily lives in fact consist of one judgment after another: "What's a good way to spend my day?" "Should I spend more time with this person or that one?" Jesus himself requires such a judgment in the very next paragraph: "Do not give dogs what is holy" (Matt. 7:6). Wait, who's a dog? Is the man who sleeps with his stepmother a dog in Paul's eyes?

In the last chapter, we thought about the outward path of the boomerang of love—how it includes and embraces. Yet the boomerang flies back—it excludes and leaves some things behind. Love, in other words, includes some things and excludes others. It draws boundaries. It weighs and assesses. It makes judgments.

What is judgment? We sometimes use the word to mean punishment. But that is only one possible outcome of judgment. Judgment is the process of assessing or weighing or measuring or evaluating whether something meets a certain standard. You might say, judging is like using a ruler. The ruler gives me the standard of an inch, and I can measure the length or width of things accordingly. That's what judgment is: measuring something against a standard.

Think of the scene in Mary Poppins when Mary takes out her tape measure and measures the children Michael and Jane. She holds the tape up to Michael and says, "Just as I thought, 'Extremely Stubborn and Suspicious.'" His sister Jane laughs until she's measured as "Rather Inclined to Giggle and Doesn't Put Things Away." Mary Poppins herself measures as "Practically Perfect in Every Way."

Paul, likewise, offered his measurement of the man sleeping with his stepmother and concluded that the man should be removed from membership in the church. He could no longer be affirmed as a Christian, because he was unrepentant. That was Paul's *judgment*. Reverend Whitfield, on the other hand, judged himself forgiven and therefore free of the need to confess. We readers, meanwhile, judge or assess him otherwise. If there ever was a dog!

Make no mistake: every form of love, righteous or unrighteous, makes judgments. To love something, by definition, is to place a value on it, as we have seen. And that's a measurement or a judgment. It is an assessment or an evaluation regarding the beloved. Even the contra-conditional love of God for sinners depends upon God's judgment of Jesus—Jesus is assessed as worthy of a bride, whatever she might look like at the moment.

The child's love in a candy store depends on just such an evaluation, as does the love of mothers, Muslims, scientists, robbers, or the man committing suicide. Loving is a judging activity. It is inherently discriminatory. It always includes and excludes simultaneously. It makes a distinction between that which is loved and that which is not. "I love her, not her." "I'll take the chocolate, not the vanilla." "I choose death, not life." You cannot love and not judge.

In one sense, it's never quite true to say someone is unloving. What we're really saying is that the person loves the wrong thing. We are disagreeing with that person's judgment about what to love, because everyone loves something.

If you have read Augustine's famous *City of God*, you may recall that he paints the whole world as belonging to either the city of God or the city of man. The inhabitants of one most love God, and the other most love themselves. Ruling these two cities, we might say, are two different judges, God and Self. And each judge has his or her own system of weights, measurements, standards that render verdicts, like "This is precious while that is not," "This is righteous while that is not," "This is lovely while that is not."

Why God's Love and Judgment Offend Us

Not surprisingly, people often have a conflicted relationship with God's love and judgment. We love his judgment when he embraces what we embrace, but we hate it when he doesn't. Likewise, we love his judgments when he excludes what we exclude, but we are offended when he doesn't. We all include some things and exclude others because we all love.

I have enjoyed a taste of such mismatched inclusions and exclusions from two or three of my critics. For years, a number of individuals whom I have come to recognize by name have criticized me on social media for commending the practices of church membership and discipline. They believe that church membership and discipline are uniformly abusive. Then I wrote an article encouraging churches to remove pastors who abuse members. When this article hit the web, my critics suddenly found themselves agreeing with me. And on a matter of discipline! This, apparently, was disconcerting to them. One posted, "Glad to see Leeman and 9Marks are on board!" (my paraphrase), even though this is the sort of thing I've been saying all along. A couple of others decided that I must have had ulterior motives for supporting their right judgment, and so they denounced me as a hypocrite.

The point is this: when others' judgments about what to include or exclude match our own, we call them wise, righteous, or loving (unless we don't trust them and so call them hypocrites). When their judgments don't match ours, we call them unwise or unloving. It's an awfully presumptuous pattern.

How then do you think fallen humanity responds to the God-centeredness of God's love, particularly when he reveals a set of judgments in keeping with the God-centeredness of his love? Not very well.

In God's love for God, his love burns for the most exquisite beauty, for matchless moral rectitude, for universe-creating power, for perfectly measured justice, for omniscient wisdom—all embodied in perfect balance and proportion. His judgments assess and declare accordingly.

We, irrationally, would prefer that God most love things with far less weight and substance. Namely, we want him to most love our glory, or the gods we worship. The fact that he doesn't offends us. So we call him intolerant, unfair, unjust, even wicked. We say things like the following:

- "You cannot send people to hell, God. That's not fair."
- "But they are good people, God. How could you let bad things happen to them?"
- "I prayed for a husband, but you didn't give me one. I cannot trust you anymore."

We assume that our judgments must be right and that his must be wrong. So we're offended.

Just as God's love and judgments offend us, so too his gospel offends us. After all, the gospel of justification by faith alone through grace alone leaves us with nothing to boast in. Glory to him and not to us? No thank you.

God's church offends us, too. Why? A church consists of people who have capitulated to this offensively self-glorying God. These traitors support his regime. What about our ways and our glory?

The practices of church membership and discipline offend us because they are anticipatory acts of judgment, foreshadowing God's final judgment. "He thinks he can exclude me?" Enforcing membership boundaries is an attempt (however imperfect) to mark off two cities or domains—one with God at the center and one with us at the center. There is no middle ground between these two domains. The sight of membership borders, then, reminds fallen humanity of what churches represent—conquered territory in *our* country. "Those people are occupiers!"

Ultimately, God's love, God's gospel, and God's church offend us because we are *glory thieves*, to borrow Paul David Tripp's phrase. Tripp illustrates the point with the simple story of a young boy at a little girl's fifth-year birthday party. The boy looks down at his small bag of party favors and then over at her mountain of gifts. Bothered by the comparison, he crosses his arms, juts out his lower lip, and utters an audible *humph!* One of the mothers at the party leans down, draws his face toward her own, and says something profound: "Johnny, it's not your party!"[3]

What's true of five-year-olds is true of us all: we treat life as if it's *our* party. We want the mountain of gifts and the kudos to belong to us, not to someone else. Not even to God. Our lives are spent conspiring toward this selfish end.

Yet, as we saw in the last chapter, bowing down to God's love for God—submitting to his glory—means being incorporated into it, sharing in it, and enjoying the most beautiful of beauties forever.

God's Judgment Makes Sense of the Universe

People rightly recognize that God's judgment in the Bible, in one sense, leads to bad news. His judgment declares that we all have sinned, and that "the wages of sin is death" (Rom. 6:23). What we miss, however, is that the Bible actually presents God's judgment as good news before it presents it as bad news. How could that be?

To judge, I've said, is to measure. Take away judgment and you effectively consign life to worthlessness. John Lennon imagined a world with no heaven or hell. He should have read Ecclesiastes. Set "under the sun," it describes Lennon's world. What the inspired poet discovered, however, is that removing the eternal measuring tape of God's

3. Paul David Tripp, *Instruments in the Redeemer's Hands: People in Need of Change Helping People in Need of Change* (Phillipsburg, NJ: P&R, 2002), 34.

judgment turns life into a nihilistic garbage ball of meaninglessness, because none of the judgments we encounter under the sun make sense. The wise dies just like the fool (2:16). The courts render unjust verdicts just like the street (3:16). The righteous receive what's due to the wicked, and the wicked receive what's due to the righteous (8:14). Good people lose elections while shameful people win (10:7). And an honest day's work will kill you (10:9). Welcome to a world with little mind for heaven or hell.

So few of the measurements or judgments of this world turn out as they should: "Under the sun the race is not to the swift, nor the battle to the strong, nor bread to the wise, nor riches to the intelligent, nor favor to those with knowledge, but time and chance happen to them all" (9:11).

Ta-Nehisi Coates, reflecting on the evils of World War II, observes that one often expects history to exact a price on injustices and evils done. But often no price is exacted from those who commit great evils. History just moves on. There is no righteousness and justice. "Indeed, much of our history is the story of things just not working out."[4]

If we're speaking about life under the sun, the author of Ecclesiastes agrees with Coates. So often life down here only leaves us with "whys." Why did God give this good woman a harsh husband? Why did this kind man get trampled on? Why does this innocent child have to suffer? Why are these godly people persecuted? Why does his hard work go unnoticed? Why does this man who wants to be married have to be alone?

It doesn't make sense. Life is not supposed to measure out like that. It all feels so futile, vain, meaningless. And that leads to despair and grief, says the author of Ecclesiastes (2:17–20).

Salvation from all this futility and meaninglessness and despair shows up in the last two verses of Ecclesiastes, and it arrives in the form of God's judgment. The author looks back at twelve chapters of frustrated judgments and then pronounces this: "The end of the matter; all has been heard. Fear God and keep his commandments, for this is the whole duty of man. For God will bring every deed into judgment, with

---

4. Ta-Nehisi Coates, "Hope and the Historian," *The Atlantic* (website), December 10, 2015, https://www.theatlantic.com/politics/archive/2015/12/hope-and-the-historian/419961/.

every secret thing, whether good or evil" (12:13–14). How is this good news? Because we can rest assured that, one day, God's judgment will right this world's inverted and senseless measurements. This is the good news that comes before the bad news.

Judgment day is that glorious day when all of history will suddenly make sense, and we will discover the true measure of everything as it's held up to the standard of God's glory. God will use his tape measure, his ruler, his scale, and things will measure rightly. We will see, for the first time, the true size and shape of justice and righteousness, as well as the true size and shape of ourselves and everyone who impacted our lives. We will see what God was doing by giving this good woman a harsh husband; why he let this kind man get trampled on; why he let this child suffer; what he accomplished by letting these godly people be persecuted.

Page by page, we will go though the books of history as recorded from heaven's perspective, and the judgments and measurements of God will be read out for every deed, with every secret thing, good or evil. Our entire lives, every moment, will be reinterpreted. God will measure every deed, and we will finally grasp their eternal significance according to his perfect standards of justice.

Apart from God's final judgment, this universe makes no sense. Everything is worthless. Nothing is precious or valuable or worthwhile. Just ask the nihilist.

God's judgment is what gives life value, meaning, and worth. It makes things precious and worthy of love. Yes, bad news will follow the good news of his judgment, namely, that we too stand condemned (apart from grace). Yet the solution is not to throw out his judgment. To despise God's judgments is to be the math student who gets angry at math when he gets a problem wrong, as if the math were being unfair. His anger works against the very structure of the universe. Talk about futility!

Hell and the Glory of God

Even hell, that worst of all punishments meted out by God's judgment, shows us the glory of God's love and the wonder of life. In all our thinking about God's love and judgment and glory, hell is like the foundation beneath a skyscraper. Pour shallow foundations and your building won't reach very high.[5]

Is God's glory weighty? His presence unimaginable? His love beyond reckoning? The unimaginable horror of hell provides an inverse measurement of all this, like the cement and steel piles sunk deep beneath the Burj Khalifa, the world's tallest building, built upon the sands of Dubai. The medieval theologian Anselm once said that a sin against an infinite God requires an infinite punishment. That might sound a little too mathematical to some, but Anslem's instincts were right. If God is something glorious, then an offense against him is something voluminous, and the magnitude of punishment shows it. Shed blood requires shed blood, says the proportionally precise author of Genesis (9:6). Why? It affirms the *worth* of the victim.

Wrath reveals worth. My siblings and I discovered at a young age, for instance, that lying to our parents yielded a stronger penalty than squabbling over a toy. Why? The truth is worth more than toys. The more precious the reality, the more terrible the consequences. Every jewelry store owner will tell you the same. Indeed, even misplaced wrath reveals what the heart actually values.

Why does Scripture offer such sobering images of hell—undying worms and unquenchable fire? Because sin dulls our senses, shrinks our horizons, and anesthetizes us to the poignancy of reality. The doctrine of hell wakes us up to a much bigger, grander universe, like moving from a world drawn in stick figures on paper to the real world. Life is more precious, the stakes are higher, and God's love and glory are greater than you ever imagined.

God Tasks Churches with Declaring His Judgments

All of God's judgments are good and right. Our fallen selves don't recognize the good because our fallen loves demand different judgments.

It's as if humanity, hired as a store manager, entered God's store, called creation, and changed all his price tags, stamping on every item a

---

5. The material in this section originally appeared in Jonathan Leeman, "Response to John Franke," in *Four Views on the Church's Mission*, ed. Jason S. Sexton (Grand Rapids, MI: Zondervan, 2017), 137–38.

price sticker out of sync with the value and price assigned by God at the store's grand opening. The cheap becomes costly and the costly becomes cheap. Remember the upside-down judgments in Ecclesiastes?

God therefore sent his apostles and prophets to walk around the store of creation, quill in hand, and record in their little book the original and true price of things. What does sex outside marriage really cost? What about neglecting my children for the sake of my career? Or looking after my elderly parents? Or caring for the downtrodden? Check the Book. It will tell you the real prices. The foolishness of God, it says, is wiser than the wisdom of men. And the weakness of God is stronger than the strength of men.

Scripture is filled with corrected price tags. The person without the Spirit will spend his entire life to buy this world, but Scripture warns that it profits a man nothing to gain the world yet forfeit his soul. The fallen woman spends her days running around asking, "What shall we eat?" or "What shall we drink?" or "What shall we wear?" But Scripture teaches her to seek first the kingdom of God and his righteousness. The fallen person seeks the praise of men; Scripture says to seek the reward that comes from the Father in heaven. The world values worldly wealth; the Book, poverty of spirit. The world, laughter; the Book, mourning. The world, self-righteousness; the Book, meekness.

So Jesus gave this job to churches: "Open up the Book. Declare the true value of things—my judgments. And conform your individual and corporate judgments to mine."

A church is almost like a curiosity shop in town whose store window features exotic items with price tags that defy immediate explanation. If you've seen enough movies, you can picture a crack in the space-time continuum opening up while a city sleeps, and such a shop being zapped into place. People wake up, walk to work as on any other day, casually look over their shoulders, and—What's that? A new store? In the storefront window they behold the judgments of God. Some will go inside. Some will throw bricks.

A church's job, in short, is to declare and to conform its members' lives to the judgments of heaven. Churches are heavenly judgment presenters. Where on earth do you go to hear and see God's judgments? To a faithful, gospel-preaching church. It's a place and people, of course, who will provoke the world's opposition. The world's people still love the false price tags. They want to wear what everyone else is wearing, do what everyone else is doing. A few, however, will realize that they have stumbled upon the beginning of eternity.

How exactly does a church declare and enact God's judgments?

The church's preaching declares his judgments. It says all humanity falls under a holy God's wrath, and then it points to the way of pardon—the good news that follows the bad news that follows the good news. For those who take that way, a church's preaching maps out the paths of wisdom and righteousness.

The church's prayers of praise, confession, and thanksgiving, too, signify its agreement with the judgments of God. We acknowledge who he is, who we are, and what he has given through Christ. Even our prayers of intercession, when aligned with his Word and Spirit, demonstrate that our ambitions have been conformed to God's judgments.

The church's singing, too, is that act of repeating his judgments back to him and to one another in a melodic and emotionally engaged fashion.

The church's two ordinances, baptism and the Lord's Supper, present preliminary judgment concerning who belongs to Christ's kingdom and who does not. They draw the lines of membership. They make the invisible church visible, showing who represents Jesus and who does not. Simultaneously, they declare who remains under God's judgment. This is what Paul did when instructing the Corinthians to hand over to Satan the man sleeping with his stepmother, and "not even to eat with such a one" (1 Cor. 5:5, 11). The man was to be excommunicated, or excluded from communion.

Finally, we "put on" his judgments in our lives throughout the week, both in times together and when apart. Our fellowship and extensions of it should picture our agreement with the judgments of God as we *include* righteousness and *exclude* unrighteousness. Every member should live as an anticipatory presentation of God's judgments.

That, ultimately, is what we call the worship of a church. As others have observed, a church's worship is its agreement with the judgments of God. We worship when we pronounce in word or deed, whether eating or drinking, singing or praying, "You, oh Lord, are worthy and precious and valuable. The idols are not."

To be clear, the pronouncements of the organized church are different from the pronouncements of individual church members at home Sunday night or throughout the week. Both a church and an individual member might say, "This is the gospel," and they might use the exact same words. The difference is that the church speaks for every member and therefore binds every member, like a judge rendering a verdict that binds the defendant. An occupant of the courtroom retelling the judge's pronouncement later in the day does not bind. The church's pronouncements, in other words, represent *the sanctioned agreement* that every member jointly affirmed when joining the church. Its version of the gospel is the "official" version, at least for the members of that church. It is the agreement of the "two or three" gathered in Jesus's name. Often, you can find that agreement written down as a statement of faith and church covenant. We will return to this idea in the next chapter.

Blurring the Lines and Obscuring God's Judgments

Regrettably, many churches today fail to grasp their role as the place on earth where God's judgments are declared and enacted in preliminary fashion. They blur the line between church and world, in the name of love. They theorize about "centered set" churches or "belonging before believing," or argue that church membership is unbiblical. Meanwhile, they seldom, if ever, confront sin. Equally, they refuse to say who belongs to the holy temple of the Lord and who doesn't. Paul tells the Corinthians to "go out from their midst, and be separate" because "we are the temple of the living God" (2 Cor. 6:16–17). These churches seem to miss the evangelistic and discipling power of making that temple concretely visible by naming a people as "the saints," "the disciples," "the forgiven ones."

The goal of such misguided churches is to lower barriers, certainly an impulse with biblical backing (1 Corinthians 9). But they remove the stumbling blocks that shouldn't be removed by obscuring God's judgment. "You might be in; you might be out. Who can say? Don't worry about it. Not a big deal." It's almost as if they don't *want* people to think about the last judgment. Or they think people are more likely to purchase a "gospel" that is all *inclusion* and no *exclusion*. Of course, that is a false gospel. Good news with no bad news before it is not, after all, good.

If there is indeed a final and great chasm, which none may cross, between the hoarding rich man and the poor man Lazarus, who lay at his gates, why would we not foreshadow that divide now by identifying the church on earth (see Luke 16:19–31)? Why would we pretend no chasm exists by letting people casually wander in and out, unnamed, unaccountable, and (finally) unloved?

Granted, churches make mistakes about who should be "in" and who should be "out." Consider Reverend Whitfield! But even then, the categories of "in" and "out of" God's kingdom are real. And even our imperfect practices press that lesson home.

Abandoning the practices of membership and discipline overlooks the evangelistic power of exclusion, to say nothing of the biblical pattern (e.g. Matt. 18:15–17; 1 Corinthians 5). Paul, however, saw no conflict between characterizing the Corinthians as "ambassadors of reconciliation" and simultaneously calling them to separate themselves as a people (see 2 Cor. 5:20; 6:17). The evangelistic power of exclusion is the power of salt and light. It's the power of distinctness. People see something different that they don't have, and they want it. What good is salt that has lost its saltiness, or light hidden beneath a bowl?

To be sure, the evangelistic power of exclusion doesn't work for the wealthy, happy, and satisfied—those who love the darkness. It works for the poor in spirit, the meek, and those hungering and thirsting for righteousness. It works for those who have begun to discover, like the author of Ecclesiastes, the futility of human judgment. Now they want something different, distinct, powerful, transformative. What is that I see through the shop window?

How the Church's Judgments Reveal God's Love

Love always depends upon a judgment, and our judgments reveal our loves. As such, the judgments of a church, insofar as they are aligned with God's, reveal the love of God.

A church's decisions about what to preach, teach, sing, and pray reveal the love of God. So do its decisions about where to spend money and whom to hire. As do its decisions about whom to baptize and remove from the Lord's Table as an act of discipline. All of these are acts of judgment, and therefore they say something about God's love. The only question is whether they line up with the judgments of God as revealed in his Word. If not, they're teaching about someone else's love.

God's judgments are often unexpected. Jesus came for the sick, not the healthy; the last, not the first. Paul wanted to boast in his weakness, not his strength. Peter talked about suffering for righteousness' sake. The author of Hebrews said we live by faith in things unseen, waiting for a city whose architect and builder is God. Most profoundly of all, the whole Bible teaches that God justifies us by our faith, not our deeds. That's the last thing our self-justifying, boastful hearts expect.

Membership

Consider a church's membership decisions. Church membership, in the strictest sense, is the *affirmation* and *oversight* a church gives to a believer's profession of faith. That is what we are doing when we baptize someone "into the name" of Christ, or when we "partake of the one bread" and declare ourselves to be "one body" (Matt. 28:19; 1 Cor. 10:17). We say to the onlooking nations, "We as a church affirm that Joe belongs to Jesus and is a member of Christ's body." We are declaring locally and visibly—in time and space—what we believe to be true universally and invisibly. It is a corporate affirmation of God's love.

These judgments sometimes look unexpected. We embrace those who are not wise according to worldly standards, not powerful, not of noble birth. We know, after all, that God chose what is foolish in the world to shame the wise, the weak to shame the strong, so that no one might boast in the presence of God (1 Cor. 1:26–29). We also welcome those who once practiced sexual immorality, idolatry, adultery, homosexuality, theft, greed, drunkenness, reviling, and swindling, but have now repented of these sins.

Think carefully, for instance, about what a church is doing when it brings a repentant swindler into membership, while excluding the salesman who continues to make a living by lying to people. It is drawing a line between the love of God and the love of the world. It is saying, "God loves honesty and fair trading and humility; he hates dishonesty and exploiting people's needs and pride." That church's membership judgment defines God's love for the world.

On one occasion, a registered sex offender sought membership in our church. He was entirely forthcoming about his past. However, the particular nature of his crime made a number of people understandably nervous. On the one hand, we wanted to love and protect the vulnerable among us. On the other hand, we wanted to proclaim that Jesus will forgive and love even people who have done what this man had done. The church decided to admit this man, upon condition that he would submit to a number of accountability structures. He happily agreed. In that situation, the church rendered a judgment that tried to show love both for a repentant sinner and for the vulnerable. In that, I hope, we revealed something more about God's love.

Discipline

Church discipline also reveals and defines God's love. The author of Hebrews reminded his readers that the Lord disciplines those he loves. His discipline shows we are true sons and daughters, he said.

How does discipline show love? Discipline, whether God's directly or a church's, draws a line between the holy and unholy, just like its membership decisions, but it does this by correcting sin. It says: "That thing you're tempted to consider so precious and valuable is not. In fact, it has no life in it at all." Discipline distinguishes between the precious and the wasteful, life and death, love and hate.

I recall a fellow member once pointing to specific areas of selfishness in my life. That was a loving act of discipline. She drew a line between the holy (unselfishness) and the unholy (selfishness) as it showed up visibly in me.

Or I think of an occasion when our church removed a man from membership who had left his wife and children for another woman. For several months we sought his repentance, but he never turned back. Therefore, we drew a line between him and the church, God's temple, by removing him from membership. We understood this to be what Jesus commands us to do in Matthew 18:15–17, as does Paul in 1 Corinthians 5. We could no longer be confident he belonged to that temple because his life suggested he prized his loves and judgments more than God's. We did not presume to possess Holy Spirit X-ray vision. We couldn't see his soul and say with absolute certainty that he was a non-Christian. We only knew that we as a church, collectively, could no longer affirm this man's profession of faith with any integrity. So we removed that affirmation rather than continue to say something we no longer believed.

The author of Hebrews also says that God disciplines us "for our good, that we may share his holiness." He continues, "For the moment all discipline seems painful rather than pleasant, but later it yields the peaceful fruit of righteousness to those who have been trained by it" (Heb. 12:10–11). The psalmist also observes,

> Blessed is the man whom you discipline, O Lord,
> and whom you teach out of your law. (Ps. 94:12)

Do you want the fruit of peace and righteousness and happiness for yourself and your church? If not, never mind discipline.

I remember the first time I took a pair of trimmers to a rose bush in my front yard. It didn't feel right. It made me nervous. "Am I really supposed to cut these branches off? Won't this hurt the plant?" But I went ahead and trimmed—on faith. A year later—lo and behold—the bush overflowed with blossoms.

In short, we discipline for the sake of love, holiness, health, and growth. A church's membership and discipline judgments define love for the world. They define it for the individuals brought in and the individuals left out. They are like a label maker, attaching labels to the city of God and the city of man, those two cities symbolizing love of God and the love of self.

Like an outstretched finger, these judgments pronounce, "Love, that way!" so that all eyes look up and see Love himself.

Evangelism and Good Deeds

The manner in which a church decides to give itself to evangelism and good deeds speaks volumes about the judgment and love of God. Do members share the gospel? Do they call people to repentance? Do they warn of his coming judgment? What kind of emphasis do the leaders place on evangelism, and what role does it play in their own lives?

Suppose, on the one hand, that the leaders of a church seldom speak of God's judgment and seldom model evangelism for the church. The members of that church, in turn, will scarcely share the gospel with family members, friends, and neighbors. Clearly that church will be saying something (false) about the nature of God's judgments and love. Suppose, on the other hand, that the pastors often feature evangelistic prayer requests, often encourage the members to share the gospel, often share the gospel in the presence of members, often speak of the coming judgment of God. That church will clearly be communicating something very different about God's love.

Likewise, the manner in which a church teaches on, prays about, and pursues being good and doing good outside the church will help define God's love for the world. Does the pastor pray on Sunday for hurting people whose stories were in the previous week's news? Do the pastors offer "platform time" to members who want to share about particular service opportunities and to ask for prayer? Do members seek ways to serve and care and give when no one is looking? The presence or absence of these kinds of activities will say something about whether God is a God of compassion and justice. Does he care for the downtrodden, the oppressed, the discriminated against?

Fellowship

Finally, consider how the smaller day-to-day judgments the members of a church must make reveal and define God's love for the world. Member Jim, who is white, speaks insensitively on a racial matter to member Jeremy, who is black. Jeremy, at that moment, must make a couple of judgments: "Should I say something to Jim and, if so, what?" If Jeremy does speak up, Jim too must make a judgment: "How will I respond to someone whose experience is different than mine?"

The elders nominate Douglas for the office of elder. Melony cannot point to anything concrete that would disqualify Douglas, but she believes he is arrogant and insensitive and shouldn't be an elder. She must now make several judgments: "How confident am I in my opinion of Douglas? What should I say to him or to the elders? Should I make my case to other members, even at the risk of being divisive?"

In social settings, member Sarah speaks continually about her athletic and academically successful children. The children of her friend Tanisha struggle in most categories, and Tanisha finds herself increasingly annoyed at Sarah and jealous. Her Bible study leader encourages her to forbear, let love cover a multitude of sins, and forgive Sarah, even if Sarah remains oblivious to her insensitivity. Tanisha has a judgment to make: "Should I just avoid Sarah, say something to her, or take my friend's counsel and quietly forgive and forbear?"

Member Gary has been out of work for a year but shows no interest in finding another job and spends all day watching television. Meanwhile, member Susanne, a single mom, works two jobs and still cannot make ends meet. Both have struggled to keep up with their rent and have now received eviction warnings. The church has two judgments to make: "How shall we help him? How can we help her?"

The Browns know that their busy schedule permits them to invite people to dinner only once a week. They think through different categories of people in the church: good friends whose company they naturally enjoy, the elderly, singles, college students, young families, people of different ethnicities or incomes, and so on. They have a judgment to make: "Whom should we prioritize?"

Each one of these judgments gives the members of a church the opportunity to reveal the love of God. That's not to say there would be one right answer to each of these questions. But in moments like these we can strive to live in accordance with the love and judgment of God or not. The passage of Scripture I have in mind comes from Jesus: "A new commandment I give to you, that you love one another: just as I have loved you, you also are to love one another. By this all people will know that you are my disciples, if you have love for one another" (John 13:34–35).

Notice, first, that the decisions we make about loving one another (or not) will display (or fail to) the love of Jesus for sinners. Notice, second, that our neighbors and non-Christian friends will know we belong to Jesus not only by how we love them but also by how we love each other.

In other words, Jeremy's decision to correct sin and Jim's decision to receive it, Douglas's nomination for the eldership and Melony's response to it, Tanisha's decision about how to respond to Sarah, and so forth all confront them with this question: will they love the other people in question as Christ has loved them?

Conclusion

Earlier in this chapter I mentioned how often people say, "Don't judge me." Whether spoken in self-defense or meant as a joke, it makes sense in a culture that's convinced itself that people can refrain from making judgments. Of course, that is impossible. We all make judgments all day. It's called decision making.

We tell ourselves we don't like the idea of judgment, of course, because judgment always involves excluding something, and someday that something just might be us. Therefore, the contemporary Western solution is to exclude exclusion. We tear down whatever walls we can. We make fun of the old traditions, like a television show that laughs at anyone who takes himself too seriously. We dispense with moral boundaries, blur gender, topple every authority we can find.

What's left? Our tribes, our idols, and our appetites. Bereft of older virtues like honor, civility, and charity, as well as the ability to think morally in general, we rely on the courts and the legislators to settle our disputes. And even they bear witness to a growing moral confusion.

In such an environment, churches are indeed like curiosity shops. How increasingly strange they look. They're filled with a group of people who actually believe "God says." And what "God says" they actually hear—and believe and obey—as love.

Which raises the question of our final chapter: What does authority have to do with love?

7

Love and Authority

It is not merely judgment we are afraid of. It's people making judgments that bind us. That brings us to the topic of authority. An authority is someone with the right to make judgments that bind others.

Authority is not the same thing as power. Power is ability, like the strength to lift a rock. At a young age you might have the power or ability to drive a car, but you do not possess the authority to do so until you have a learner's permit or a license

Authority, again, is a moral right or a moral permission slip to make judgments and exercise power in a particular domain. It's a license or an authorization. Others inside that domain possess an obligation to obey, at least according to the terms specified in the authorization. I have to obey the policeman about the speed limit; I don't have to obey him about whom to marry.

To use another example: a father possesses authority over his children; they fall within his domain. Yet his authority is limited because he, in turn, is under a higher moral authority. He does not possess an absolute right to do with them as he pleases. God never authorizes fathers to exasperate or harm their children. No father possesses that authority. Rather, his authority over his children must always remain within the terms specified by the authorizer, God.

God alone has absolute, unquestionable authority. His authority *is*. He can, when he wants, tell us what to eat, what to wear, whom to sleep with. His authority is not subject to judicial review or a job termination, because we didn't put him in office. We might ignore him for a while, but we cannot vote him out. He possesses an intrinsic moral right to rule, make judgments, exercise power. Like an author who writes whatever he pleases, so the author of all creation has all authority over what he has made.

Human authority, however, is always relative and limited. It's not something we *are*. It's something we must *be given*.[1] It's an office we must step into—whether parent, husband, citizen, church member, pastor/elder, policeman, congressman, judge, teacher, airline pilot, toll-booth operator, or other. Our authority is borrowed from God, which means God always sets its limits and purposes.

Those are some of the definitional basics on authority. They're pretty straightforward. But the drama of authority—ah, that's a different thing. And what drama there is!

At least two things create the drama. First, we all want to wield authority, at least over ourselves. There's an impulse inside us all, when crossed, to react: "*You* are not God! *You* have no right. Who do *you* think you are?" All of us are spring-loaded to jump to battle when the boots of others trespass into our territory.

Second, we know all too well how often authority is abused. Parents abuse their children; ministers defraud their congregations; bosses discriminate against classes of workers; political leaders take bribes; the powerful prey on the weak. So we decide authority cannot be trusted. It's like a gun. You don't just leave one lying around the house. Someone is going to get shot. In fact, maybe we should get rid of the gun altogether.

So what do we do with authority? It seems essential for coordinating the lives of people together. You can't just let anyone drive a car, for example. But is authority inherently unloving? If we are going to talk about authority, we have to face its more difficult realities.

An Honest Look

Toni Morrison's Pulitzer Prize–winning novel *Beloved* offers a heart-rending look at the destructive power of authority.[2] The novel is set in

1. These insights come from Nicholas Wolterstorff, *The Mighty and the Almighty: An Essay in Political Theology* (New York: Cambridge University Press, 2012), 48.

2. Although slavery certainly did not possess a legitimate *moral* sanction, it did possess an unjust, evil legal sanction, which is why I think the term *authority* remains the right word and not just *power*.

1874 in the aftermath of slavery. It deals with the ongoing social and psychological impact of slavery on several freed blacks.

In one scene, a grandmother figure named Baby Suggs reflects on why she's not worried about the possibility of her youngest son's death. She realizes that she "had been prepared for that better than she had for his life." After all, her white owners had stolen every one of her children away from her. So she had learned not to take an interest in them.

> The last of her children . . . she barely glanced at when he was born because it wasn't worth the trouble to try to learn features you would never see change into adulthood anyway. Seven times she had done that: held a little foot; examined the fat fingertips with her own—fingers she never saw become the male or female hands a mother would recognize anywhere.

Can you imagine having seven children stolen? By legal authority? By constitutional sanction? As property? What does this do to a mother?

> She didn't know to this day what their permanent teeth looked like; or how they held their heads when they walked. Did Patty lose her lisp? What color did Famous' skin finally take? Was that a cleft in Johnny's chin or just a dimple that would disappear soon's his jawbone changed? Four girls, and the last time she saw them there was no hair under their arms. Does Ardelia still love the burned bottom of bread? All seven were gone or dead. What would be the point of looking too hard at that youngest one?[3]

Tender children. Sold to an unknown master. To use and abuse as he pleased.

Yet it wasn't just her children she didn't know. Baby Suggs, upon gaining her freedom, realized she didn't know herself.

> Sad as it was that she did not know where her children were buried or what they looked like if alive, fact was she knew more about them than she knew about herself, having never had the map to discover what she was like. Could she sing? (Was it nice to hear when she

3. Toni Morrison, *Beloved* (New York: Vintage, 2004), loc. 2276–78, Kindle.

> did?) Was she pretty? Was she a good friend? Could she have been a loving mother? A faithful wife? Have I got a sister and does she favor me? If my mother knew me would she like me?[4]

We become who we are through our relationships—lover, friend, mother, wife, sister, daughter. Slave masters seemed to know instinctively that severing these bonds would dehumanize the slave and convert him or her into a more useful tool: a garden spade, a cooking mitt, a water bucket, a field plow. Baby Suggs had been treated not as the image of God but as a tool all her life.

Legally sanctioned power—authority—extinguished the human in the human.

In the face of these realities, might not any blithe and chirpy affirmation that "authority is loving" seem naïve? Might it not risk promoting more injustice?

The title of the book *Beloved* is rich with irony. I won't take the time to explain its role in the novel, other than to say that love tries hard to exist throughout the book. It reaches desperately for an opportunity. Grabs at hope. Wants to live. But 1874 remains utterly haunted by the past. It's not as if the chains came off and suddenly the slaves were happy, healthy people. Slavery's destructive power continued inside them. The characters in the novel, tragically, are capable of only warped and self-defeating versions of love. Just when you think two of them might enjoy love's embrace—a mother and a daughter, a man and a woman, a girl and her sister—the "tangled jungle" inside of each character spoils the attempt and leaves the person empty-handed. The quotations above offer a glimpse into the psychology of how mind-destroying such abuses of power can be. People never recover from some abuses. The injuries never go away, at least on this side of glory.

With all this in mind, again we ask, can love and authority coexist? Understandably, many think the answer must be no. Our age is happy to offer therapy and encouragement and redirection. Disruptive children in a classroom might need these things, but not discipline. The word *discipline* sounds too hard, too authoritarian.

4. Morrison, *Beloved*, loc. 2293–97, Kindle.

But is that right? In fact, I think authority is essential for life and growth. There is a difference between a good use of authority and an abusive use, which is authoritarianism.

Or, to put it even more strongly, I don't think we can actually separate love and authority, just as I said we cannot separate love and judgment in the last chapter. There I said the link between love and judgment is inevitable, because love always depends upon a judgment. So it is with authority. We all use whatever authority we have been given for the purposes of our loves—every time. This is true of the Abraham Lincolns and the Adolf Hitlers, a company's boss and a babysitter, you and me. Love rules. That's what love does. Love always employs whatever dominion it possesses for its purposes.

The real question in our use of authority is, what or whom do we most love? That's whose rule we will establish. Remember Augustine's two cities. We either love God most or love ourselves most, and our love will work toward one of those two ends. We will work either for God's life-creating glory or for our own universe-shrinking power.

Churches, for their part, should be pictures of one and not the other. They are to be embassies of heaven where the love of God rules. His loving rule should be displayed in the authority of the congregation, its leaders, and its individual members.

To see that, let's think about authority in creation, the fall, and redemption, and then authority in a church.

Authority in Creation

Farmer Adam wakes up at 4:30 a.m., pulls on his overalls and boots, resupplies the chicken feeder, milks the cows, and then climbs onto his tractor to till a field. God has told him to "work" his farm and to "keep" it (Gen. 2:15).

It will be a long day, but the work is good and rewarding. He supplies grain, milk, and eggs for the town. Others turn the grain into bread and pasta, the milk into yogurt and cheese, and the eggs into omelets. His wife Evelyn and their children contribute their part. And the workers he hires allow him to yield the grain of three fields, not just one.

God created farmer Adam and wife Evelyn in his own image, and he assigned them to the joint task of ruling over their little plot of land. He told them to be fruitful, multiply, fill, subdue, and have dominion (Gen. 1:28). Picking up his Bible, farmer Adam realizes that being created in God's image means that he and Evelyn are a son and a daughter of God, and that they have been crowned as king and queen over their chickens, cows, children, and fields.

Yet it's not just them. All image-bearing humanity has been crowned kings and queens. The psalmist looks on with wonder:

> What is man that you are mindful of him,
>   and the son of man that you care for him?
>
> Yet you have made him a little lower than the heavenly beings
>   and crowned him with glory and honor.
> You have given him dominion over the works of your hands;
>   you have put all things under his feet,
> all sheep and oxen,
>   and also the beasts of the field,
> the birds of the heavens, and the fish of the sea,
>   whatever passes along the paths of the seas. (Ps. 8:4–8)

To be human is to be assigned rule. That's a significant part of what it means to be created in God's image. Just as a son looks and acts like his father, and does what his father does, so we were created to rule, like our God who is a King. Essential to being a human is ruling—possessing and exercising authority—in a way that reflects the character of God.

Should farmer Adam and wife Evelyn rule over their children and farm hands in the same way they do the chickens and the cows? Of course not. The children and farm workers, too, are created in God's image. They are kings and queens in their own right. That means Adam and Evelyn's task is to raise, nurture, and instruct their children like princes and princesses, preparing them for their own rule. And the farmhands should be paid fairly and given the opportunity to maximize their own potential as rulers. Maybe the three fields will multiply to nine through their industry, and each will gain charge over several. The assistants will grow into managers, and managers into owners of their own farmlands.

God grants every human a certain domain and a host of rules and regulations for stewarding that domain. Here are two of the most crucial:

First, *use your authority to create, grow, and help human flourishing. Authority* exists to *author*, as the common Latin root of the two words implies. God authored creation out of nothing. We image him by taking the something he created and giving order, shape, or function to it. So we till the dirt, plant the field, build the house, pave the roads, sell our goods in the marketplace.

Second, *use your authority over humans by equipping and authorizing them to exercise rule*. God uses his authority generously. He delegates. He empowers those made in his image, so that they can image, mirror, copy, represent him. This is why the psalmist is so astonished: he notices all the stars that God set in place and then bursts out, "What is man that you are mindful of him" (Ps. 8:4). We could never set stars in place. We might wonder why God didn't just rule the earth and subdue it without us—he'd do such a better job on his own! He could make sure no one was ever stuck in traffic, and children's shoelaces didn't end up in knots, to say nothing of war, crime, and poorly engineered bridges that collapse. Still, for his own reasons, God entrusts authority to us. He gives us space to exercise rule, grow, make mistakes, flop, and start all over. He is like a father saying to his son, "Build this tree house with me," or like a mother saying to her daughter, "Bake this cake with me," even though the parent knows the child will not do it nearly as well.

God's rule of us is nothing if not generous. He wants us to share in his glory because as we share in it, we image or display his glory for all to see. Our authority over other image bearers, whether our children or assistants in the office, should likewise seek to empower, equip, and promote. It's the teacher teaching, the coach coaching, the mother mothering. It says: "Learn more. Run faster. Love well. I'll give you the tools."

Authority, as God intended it in creation, doesn't extinguish the human in the human. The human was designed for authority, the way a race car is designed to race. That's why, when you're given the chance to exercise authority in one way or another, you'll sometimes find yourself thinking, "Yes, I was *made* to do this!" Questions of sin aside, for the moment, exercising authority is properly gratifying and enlivening.

Yet that's not just about exercising control. It's also about loving and serving others. Good authority works not just from the top down but also from the bottom up. Picture me at Disneyland, one daughter on my shoulders, another in hand, and chasing the third and fourth around the park doing all I can to please them. Or picture my wife driving from ballet practice to softball practice to piano practice. Like the authority of God, who is the "rock" on which we stand, so loving authority in creation is often about laying your life down as a platform on which others build their lives. That's what I mean when I say it's not just top-down; it's also bottom-up. "I'll supply you, fund you, resource you, guide you"—bottom-up. Yet also, "Here are the rules"—top down. It's both.

Good authority binds in order to loose, corrects in order to teach, trims in order to grow, disciplines in order to train, legislates in order to build, judges in order to redeem, studies in order to innovate. Trust me, and I will give you a garden in which to create a world. Just keep my commandments. I love you.

Good authority loves. Good authority gives. Good authority passes out authority.

God designed farmer Adam to do what he does on the farm for the purposes of love—love of God and love of neighbor. He will feed the chickens and milk the cows because he loves his wife and children. He will sow and harvest the field because he loves his workers and fellow townspeople. And he will love all of them because they are created in God's image, and he loves God most of all. In a lesser way, he will even love the soil of the earth as a gift from God, the way one might love a car or a house. So he will adopt sustainable farming practices. Yet his purpose here is always to serve people and God, so that they might better know God.

Godly authority or rule, quite simply, is the *operation of love*. It's what the furnace of godly affections does. It's the teacher teaching because he wants his students to know the beauty of God's world. It's the coach coaching because he wants his players to know the joy of glorifying God with their skill and determination. It's the mother mothering because she wants her children to love the Lord with their hearts, souls, and minds. Holy love is the ground for every godly and good use of authority. It provides authority's purpose and framework.

Authority Fallen

One day, however, farmer Adam wakes up with a headache. He lets himself sleep a little longer, hoping the headache might go away. When he does get up, he feels anxious about the schedule, so he barks at his children. He doesn't thank and encourage his wife for her work but lets her hear him grumbling under his breath. Soon he finds himself shouting at his workers, accusing them of slacking off. The process repeats itself for a number of days, then weeks. The workers trust him less. They work hard only when he's looking and compete against each another for his favor. They even sabotage one another's work. Downhill the whole farm goes.

What happened? For starters, farmer Adam stopped loving God first and began to love himself first. He became preoccupied with his schedule, his plans, his control, his sense of rightness. This meant, second, that he began to define justice and righteousness around his own perceptions and impulses. And this meant, third, he was disobeying God. God charged farmer Adam with loving and showing kindness toward everyone around him. He charged him to not exasperate his children and to care for workers beneath him. Yet farmer Adam decided, at least during his outbursts, that his own law was uppermost, not God's. Fourth and finally, he began to view his wife, children, and workers less as God-imagers and more as tools to be employed for his purposes. You might say he dehumanized them, even if only slightly.

Authoritarianism or abuse dehumanizes people and uses them for one's own ends. It treats people as tools for one's own pleasure and glory, not as God's image bearers crowned with a God-assigned glory and honor.

History teaches the same lesson. The great atrocities recorded in the history books, such as American slavery mentioned above, typically involve dehumanizing one's victims before enslaving, torturing, or killing them. So observes David Livingstone Smith in his book, *Less Than Human: Why We Demean, Enslave, and Exterminate Others*. The average Nazi convinced himself that killing Jews was okay by rationalizing that Jews were dangerous and disease-carrying "rats." The Hutus of Rwanda regarded the Tutsi as "cockroaches" and clubbed them to death by the hundreds of thousands. White Americans called Native Americans "savages" and African Americans "property" in order to justify rape, manstealing, and the piles of corpses. On and on the historical record reads, all the way back to ancient Chinese, Egyptian, and Mesopotamian literature.

It's hard to kill or enslave your own kind, Livingston says. It's easier to kill something subhuman, especially by systematic and legally sanctioned means. A murderous regime doesn't only need power; it also needs some way to feel better about the atrocious acts it commits. It needs a moral argument or a rationalization, the kind you may have learned at age four when reprimanded for hitting your brother: "But he took my truck!"

Jumping to our own day, is it any wonder, then, that abortion advocates call the entity inside a woman's womb a fetus, organic tissue, uterine contents, a clump of cells, or a part of the woman's own body, like an appendix? If you want to support abortion, you certainly don't want to call it a baby or a child. The argument for abortion follows the same script as nearly every slaveholding or genocidal regime in history. Dehumanize anyone who gets in the way of what you want or love.

Across the board, bad authority discourages, cripples, wilts, sucks dry, snuffs out, annihilates. It's always hungry for more—more territory, more control. And so it hates constraints. It believes it can loose without binding, grow without trimming, innovate without study. Yet in the process of always taking, never giving, it becomes a universe-shrinking black hole. If God's rule is generous and enlarges life, fallen human rule is selfish and implodes life. Even the leader often becomes smaller. Have you ever noticed how the circle of friends around a selfish sibling, boss, or dictator dwindles? The abuser becomes pitiful and paranoid. That is the fallout of political imperialism, economic exploitation, environmental degradation, business monopolization, social degradation, and child abuse.

Not that bad authority always wears such monstrous faces. Often it charms and persuades. It borrows truth and offers empathy. It says:

"I know how you're feeling. I recognize your troubles. Here is the solution. So listen to me. Keep *my* commandments."

The value of looking at history's greater atrocities is that they cast in broad relief what's true of all sin, even if it's just farmer Adam acting unkindly toward his wife and children. Sin, ultimately, is nothing more or less than humanity's misuse of authority—misusing the freedom of choice that God gave. Eve's bite of the fruit and Pharaoh's bloodshed belong to the same class, operate by the same principles, possess the same authorization. The DNA is the same. Pharaoh just swung a much bigger hammer.

Fallen authority takes a good and glorious gift that God has given to humanity and employs it for evil. It is a liar and a charlatan. Yet it is so very real, at least for a time.

Authority Redeemed

Gratefully, farmer Adam and wife Evelyn go to church one Sunday, hear the good news of Jesus Christ, repent, and put their trust in Christ.

He returns to his farm that afternoon determined to lead as Jesus would have him. He thinks of Jesus's words about not "lord[ing] it over" others and about coming "not to be served but to serve" (Mark 10:42, 45). He considers the picture of Jesus bearing a crown of thorns, donning the robe of mockery, and mounting the throne of the cross. Jesus, he realizes, ruled by giving up his life as a ransom for many. He imaged God's love and authority perfectly. He didn't crush the human in the human, but re-created, authored, empowered, and commissioned the human. He inaugurated a whole new creation. He then sent his Spirit to help his followers become fully human. Farmer Adam wonders, what does it take to exercise leadership and authority as a follower of Christ?

We need to focus on at least three words in answer to that question: *love, submission,* and *faith.*

Love

Recall, first, what love is. It's affectionately affirming that which is from God in the beloved, and giving oneself to seeing God exalted in the beloved. So Jesus came into the world and loved his disciples "to the end" (John 13:1). He gave himself to God and to his people, that God might be exalted in their lives. He taught with authority, commanded wind and seas, subjected the demons and bound Satan, claimed authority to forgive sins, accepted the worship of his disciples, and professed to possess all authority in heaven and on earth. No one else has ever held such authority. And yet he did all this for love's sake—love of God and love of neighbor.

We, too, must wield every scrap of authority God gives us for love's sake—toward God and neighbor. This is true whether God establishes us as police officers or parents, voters or vice-presidents of marketing. To the extent that we employ our authority for an exclusive love of self, we sin and begin to abuse and exploit others. We're back to the black hole and a shrinking universe. The logic should be clear: if I love me most, you are a tool for my glory. Yet, if I love God most, I can affectionately affirm what's from God in you and then give myself to seeing God exalted in your life.

Submission

Consider, second, the role of submission or obedience. In fact, this point might be the most overlooked of these three, so I'll spend more time on it. Godly leadership always begins with submission, or obedience, or conformity, or following. If that sounds counterintuitive, consider that Jesus submitted to the Father perfectly, and so he was granted all authority.

The principle that submission always precedes authority is rooted in our being created as God-imagers. To rule on his behalf, we must first conform ourselves to his image. We must mirror the Almighty. And as we mirror him, we do as he does: we rule. It's almost like the old movie *Dave*, in which a presidential impersonator looks so much like the president (played by the same actor, of course) that, when the real president falls into a coma, the White House staff secretly installs the impersonator. And it works: he leads as president. The analogy has its limitations, but we know that Jesus mimicked the Father, and we too should mimic God.

The act of conforming our lives to the will of God is the beginning of rule. Remember what we heard from Oliver O'Donovan earlier: "To be *in* authority, you have to be *under* it, and if you are under it you are in it."[5] We all learned this dynamic as children. Picture several children breaking the classroom rules as soon as their teacher steps out of the room. But one kid speaks up: "Teacher said we're not supposed to do that." The rest of the group becomes annoyed and calls him a "teacher's pet" or a "goodie-two-shoes." Why? Because at that moment this lone voice is submitting to the authority figure, participating in the work of the authority, and seemingly usurping that authority. Though not formally authorized, the child represents the teacher by imaging or mimicking her—which is especially annoying, provoking the backlash, "No one made you our boss!"

Why do you think your non-Christian friends sometimes resent your Christian obedience? Because your obedience represents God's rule asserting itself, by implication, in their lives. Your obedience is, paradoxically, a form of ruling.

I experienced the dynamic of submission leading to leadership in my own life. By nature, I am a nonconformist. I like to examine counterarguments to better understand the main argument, and I also like to be my own boss. Yet it was when, by God's grace, I began to submit to the pastors over me that God began to entrust me with more and more responsibility and authority in a church. Eventually I even became an elder.

Submission is the pathway to growth and leadership. How often Christians miss this, even though the example of Christ teaches it plainly.

Submission is also the pathway to fruitfulness, as Christ also teaches plainly. Think once more of the blessed man in Psalm 1. He delights in and meditates on the law of the Lord. He submits. And the result? He is like a tree planted by streams of water that yields fruit. He prospers. Submission to God's law and the authorities he has placed over us doesn't extinguish this man's life or creative potential. It multiplies it.

5. Oliver O'Donovan, *Desire of the Nations: Rediscovering the Roots of Political Theology* (Cambridge: Cambridge University Press, 1996), 90.

Not only that, but the more a leader submits himself to the law of God, the less likely he or she is to abuse those lower on the totem pole. A good leader knows he or she is constrained by God's law, constrained by the rules of his or her office, constrained to the specified objectives of that office, constrained by a profound understanding of people as God-imagers. The pastor knows he's not a prince. The parent knows she's not a policeman. Each of these is a distinct, God-established office. Each possesses its own license. When I turned sixteen and got my driver's license, I was dismayed to learn that the license did not include permission to drive a motorcycle. My authority to drive had limits. Good authority drives what God says it can drive. And it drives inside God's lanes.

Faith

Finally, consider the role of faith. Everything I've said about *love* and *submission* was present in seed form at creation and blossomed in Jesus. Though God walked with Adam and Eve in the garden, our loving rule now works by faith in an unseen God we love and obey. The fruit of our leadership is not always immediate, but often deferred. This point is critical because leadership in this world is so often gauged by visible results. And for many offices in life, that remains appropriate. Shareholders rightly concern themselves with share prices and should evaluate the leadership accordingly. Voters reward results at election time. The construction foreman manages the schedule with an end result in view.

Yet, godly leadership isn't measured only by results. It's also measured by our faithfulness in leading according to God's design. If I have a choice between illegally withholding a report about my company so that share prices don't drop and faithfully reporting it, I know that God will evaluate "success" differently than my colleagues might. This is even more the case in jobs devoted to nurturing human beings, like parenting and being a pastor. There are ways to manufacture results in these domains, but such results are usually skin deep. In fact, forcing those results on the child or the church member can be a form of abuse. Such was the abuse of the Pharisees, who thought they could get results by piling up laws. So much of godly pastoring and parenting is about planting seeds and then waiting for God to give the growth, as farmer Adam has been doing his whole career.

Farmer Adam's desire to lead like Jesus led means loving like Jesus loved, obeying like Jesus obeyed, and trusting the Father in heaven like Jesus trusted. The same is true for all of us who would exercise authority in a godly manner.

How the Church Embodies God's Love and Authority

So what's the lesson here for our churches? Well, let's start with what a church is. A church, we could say, is a group of people who embody God's love and authority in their lives together and among outsiders. It is an embassy of his rule and a garden of his love.

Farmer Adam continues to farm, but he also begins to pastor. On both weekdays and Sundays he plants seeds, but they are different kinds of seeds. On Monday through Saturday, farmer Adam sows seeds of grain. On Sunday, Pastor Adam scatters the seed of God's Word. This Word pronounces God's judgments with all authority. Sometimes that seed falls on dry soil. Those are the visitors who don't come back. Sometimes it falls on weed-filled or rocky soil. Those are the people who seem excited about church at first but soon get into trouble. And sometimes the seed falls on good soil. When it does, it takes root in the hearts of hearers and then, by God's Spirit, blossoms and grows. These hearers begin to love each other. They increasingly recognize how precious every other member is—God-imagers with Godward potential. Black, brown, white, and Asian; rich and poor; men and women; the mature and the immature—all of them are increasingly precious to each other. So they increasingly give themselves to seeing God exalted in one another's lives. Sometimes weeds must be pulled and bushes trimmed. Yet through all of this, the garden grows and flourishes.

Members of a church where love rules don't horde authority and opportunity. Instead, they look for ways to strengthen and minister to one another, so that the whole body builds itself up in love. Certainly, this means caring for one another's physical needs as occasion requires, as God cares for us. Yet, more than that, it means forgiving one another and pointing to the rule of God as set down in his Word, so that all might follow in God's ways and participate in his rule.

To preach and teach is to exercise loving authority because it points people to God's revelation. To disciple is to exercise loving authority because it seeks to see people conformed to the image of God. To evangelize is to participate in loving authority because it tells the nations that God is their Judge and King, and that he offers a way of pardon.

The fruit of these exercises is not usually seen quickly. The teaching and discipling and evangelizing work by faith. The kingdom of God, Jesus said, is like a seed scattered on the ground. The farmer sleeps and rises night and day, and the seed sprouts and grows, though he doesn't know how (Mark 4:26–27).

As on the farmland, the goal in the church is to create and nurture life—in this case, supernatural life. It's to cultivate a harvest of righteousness and peace. It's to live and grow as God's new creation.

Unity in Diversity

One particularly prominent way for the church to embody God's love and authority is through its witness of unity in diversity. Just as God's creation boasts many kinds of flowers, animals, and people, so the new-creation people will bear a glorious diversity, bound together in unity. Diversity is not a problem in need of a solution but is good in itself. It's a feature, not a bug, as the programmers say.

On the one hand, the people of God are one, and there are no distinctions among them. "Here there is not Greek and Jew, circumcised and uncircumcised, barbarian, Scythian, slave, free; but Christ is all, and in all" (Col. 3:11; see also Rom. 10:12). The members of Pastor Adam's church know they share one body, one Spirit, one hope, one Lord, one faith, one baptism (Eph. 4:4–5). Therefore, they strive to bear with one another in love, with all humility and gentleness, "eager to maintain the unity of the Spirit in the bond of peace" (Eph. 4:2–3).

On the other hand, they don't leave behind their created distinctives and their diverse experiences in a fallen world. Instead, the different categories into which human beings divide one another, both fairly and unfairly, become the occasions for God's power to create unity *in* diversity. Perhaps the best chapter in the Bible on this point is 1 Corinthians 12. Paul begins by observing the diversity of gifts given to the church, each to be used for the common good. Then he broadens what he means by diversity by drawing from different categories of people: "For just as the body is one and has many members, and all the members of the body, though many, are one body, so it is with Christ. For in one Spirit we were all baptized into one body—Jews or Greeks, slaves or free—and all were made to drink of one Spirit" (vv. 12–13). The distinction between Jew and Greek was of God. The distinction between slave and free was not. Yet Paul insists that each type of person was a member of the body, and like each part of a physical body, each member of the church needs every other member:

> For the body does not consist of one member but of many. If the foot should say, "Because I am not a hand, I do not belong to the body," that would not make it any less a part of the body. And if the ear should say, "Because I am not an eye, I do not belong to the body," that would not make it any less a part of the body. (vv. 14–16)

Instead, God has purposes for each part—Jew and Gentile, slave and free, male and female, black and white, those gifted with preaching and those gifted with administration. Each member has a way to serve the whole body: "But as it is, God arranged the members in the body, each one of them, as he chose" (v. 18).

Creation imposes its categories, like male and female. The fall imposes its categories, like slave and free. And both kinds of categories dramatically affect the lives of church members. They affect how people view themselves and relate to the world around them. They affect the gifts and sympathies members bring to the body, the stories they can tell, the songs they can sing, the hurts and sorrows they know and can share. Becoming a Christian does not suddenly erase, for instance, everything that a woman is and the experiences she has had as a woman. A black Christian is not suddenly, somehow, not black.

In light of these kinds of differences, Paul tells the Corinthians to be sensitive to each other. He also wants the Corinthians to be sensitive when differences pertain to gifts and roles. The parts that seem weaker, he says, are indispensable. On the less honorable, we bestow greater honor. There should be no division, he continues, but members should care for one another. "If one member suffers, all suffer together; if one member is honored, all rejoice together" (vv. 22–26).

Christianity is color-blind with regard to our salvation, but not with regard to the God-intended diversity of the body. A church's challenge is to demonstrate color blindness in all the right ways ("You are my brother/sister in Christ") and color consciousness in all the right ways ("You are different and wonderful and have new things to teach me"). True unity in Christ provides the security wherein diversity enlightens and delights, rather than threatens and offends.

Paul's picture of unity in diversity in this chapter dramatically impacts the politics of a church. He doesn't do away with all authority, whether of the state or of parents or of husbands or even of elders. He doesn't say all authority is bad. No, God continues to use various offices for leading his people and for all creation's good. Yet inside the church he makes our oneness in Christ primary. As such, our union and equality in him is primary. Think back to Jeremiah's new covenant promise: "And no longer shall each one teach his neighbor and each his brother, saying, 'Know the Lord,' for they shall all know me, from the least of them to the greatest, declares the Lord" (Jer. 31:34). Every member is a priest-king, and every member is equal before God.

A couple of implications follow. First, this means that every member, male or female, shares in the church's highest authority: the authority of the whole congregation. I'll return to this in a moment.

Second, any distinctions of rank or hierarchy between church members outside the church are quickly relativized and demoted in significance. Think of Paul's exhortation to Philemon concerning his runaway bond servant Onesimus. He sends Onesimus back, but he appeals "for love's sake" to Philemon to receive Onesimus "no longer as a bondservant but more than a bondservant, as a beloved brother" (Philemon 9, 16). The political distinction between master and bond servant still exists legally. Paul cannot change that. But he can tell Philemon to let go of that hierarchy and to receive Onesimus as a brother.

Here are two contemporary examples: First, I love how the one- and two-star generals in Capitol Hill Baptist Church, when I was a member there, never asked for special recognition. In fact, most people didn't know they were generals. The same was true of the individuals who held political office or ran entire government agencies. They treated others as equals and humbly welcomed being treated like everyone else.

Second, my boss and former pastor, Mark Dever, a white man, was walking through the slave quarters on a tour of Mount Vernon, the home of George Washington. Reflecting on how many American slaves were Christians, he realized that these fellow Christians were "his people" more than any of their white masters who denied Christ. His "politics" and relationships have been changed by the gospel.

The lesson for you and me is this: we are Christians before we are male or female, this ethnicity or that, this nationality or that, a member of this party or of that, the child of such and such parents, or a member of any other group this world might use to define us. Not only so, but we let Jesus redefine all those categories. "Jesus, *you* tell me what it means to be a man and how to use the fact that I'm white, or that I'm an American."

In short, the church, centered on the gospel of Jesus Christ, creates its own kind of politics, a politics of peace and righteousness and love that will confound the nations. Sometimes the nations will love, but often they will hate, the embassies of heaven known as Christian churches.[6]

Two Kinds of Authority

If churches are embassies of Christ's love and rule, we should think for a moment about the authority of the church and its leaders.

God grants human beings two different kinds of authority, and understanding them is quite helpful for knowing how to live together as churches under the leadership of pastors. The two kinds might be called *the authority of command* and *the authority of counsel*. Both kinds allow you to make commands that should be obeyed (despite their differing names). The difference is this: with an authority of command, you have

6. On this topic more broadly, see Jonathan Leeman, *How the Nations Rage: Rethinking Faith and Politics for a Divided Age* (Nashville: Nelson, 2018); and Leeman, *Political Church: The Local Assembly as Embassy of Christ's Rule* (Downers Grove, IL: IVP Academic, 2016).

the right to enforce those commands unilaterally. With the authority of counsel, you don't.

I'll try to illustrate. God gives governments and parents of young children the authority of command. He gives the state "the sword" to enforce its decisions, and he gives parents "the rod" to enforce theirs. A policeman, for instance, can enforce the speed limit by giving you a ticket. And a parent can enforce bedtime for a young child with any number of consequences.

Now, what about a husband? I believe God gives husbands authority, but I would certainly not say that God gives husbands the right to "enforce" their authority, like the state or a parent. Instead, husbands possess an authority of counsel. That authority is real because wives are biblically obligated to submit, and Jesus will hold them accountable in the final judgment (Eph. 5:22; 1 Pet. 3:1). But nowhere does the Bible give a husband the right to enforce his decisions or requests or appeals. The wife must *choose* to consent.

With this distinction between command and counsel in mind, let's think about congregations and elders or pastors. What kind of authority do they have? I won't take the time to lay out the biblical arguments here; I've done that in other books.[7] But I believe the Bible teaches that gathered congregations possess the authority of command, while elders or pastors possess the authority of counsel. If the state has "the sword" and parents have "the rod," Jesus gave the gathered congregation "the keys of the kingdom" (see Matt. 16:19; 18:17–18). The keys are the enforcement mechanism that allows churches to do things like bring people into membership, affirm their departure to another church, or discipline them from membership when necessary. The keys belong to every member, male and female, young and old, immature and mature, and are to be used when the church is gathered together (Matt. 18:20; 1 Cor. 5:4). They provide a church with its final human authority.

Meanwhile, God has given an authority of counsel to the elders or pastors, terms the Bible uses interchangeably. Pastors teach Scrip-

7. For a short, popular-level read, see Jonathan Leeman, *Understanding the Congregation's Authority* (Nashville: B&H, 2016). For a more academic treatment, see Leeman, *Don't Fire Your Church Members: The Case for Congregationalism* (Nashville: B&H Academic, 2016).

ture and give oversight to the congregation on how to use the keys. For instance, they might say, "We recommend that you receive John into membership" or "that you remove Jane from membership" or "that you affirm Joe as an elder." When they do, the author of Hebrews would say to the church, "Obey your leaders and submit to them" (13:17). The congregation should follow the elders' counsel. Is there ever a time the congregation shouldn't follow? Of course. The congregation should oppose the elders any time the elders recommend a course of action that jeopardizes the integrity, nature, or mission of the church and its doctrine.

Now, that whole discussion about two kinds of authority may or may not be interesting to you. Why did I bring it up? There are three reasons:

1. *The nature of elders' (and husbands') authority dramatically impacts how elders (and husbands) should go about exercising that authority.* Like husbands, elders should not "give orders," as an army instructor will. Elders don't have that kind of authority. Rather, their authority is more suited to teaching, appealing, and, like husbands, wooing. Like husbands, they seek to nurture, strengthen, and promote unity. For those purposes, forcing a church member into a particular decision isn't worth much, nor is twisting a wife's arm. Instead, elders should live with their congregations in an understanding way, as the Bible instruct husbands to treat wives. Elders should not "lord it over" members, just as, again, husbands shouldn't be domineering. Rather, elders must lead by pointing members to the Word of God and doing so with great patience.

It should not surprise anyone, therefore, that biblical complementarianism, the view that men and women are equal but have different and complementary roles, applies to both the church and the home. The initiating, protecting, nurturing headship of husbands in the home provides one picture of how pastors should lead their flocks. Or rather, the leadership of elders provides an example for husbands.

2. *The relationship between elder leadership and congregational authority builds a discipleship dynamic into the very structure of the church.* Remember the man who slept with his stepmother, which we discussed in chapter 6? Paul said he had rendered "judgment" on the man. But then he told the church to imitate him by rendering its own

judgment (1 Cor. 5:3, 12). Paul used his authority and then asked the church to use its own. In other words, he discipled his readers, "Do as I do." Here's the formula:

Elder leadership + congregational rule = discipleship

I sometimes call this Jesus's discipleship program.

A pastor's or elder's work is to train. It depends upon modeling and repetition in both word and deed. Speaking figuratively, an elder demonstrates how to use the hammer and saw, and then places the tools into the member's hands. He plays the piano scale or swings the golf club and then asks the member to repeat the action. "Do as I do."

Members should not regard pastors or elders as possessing "blue blood" (like the seventeenth-century aristocracy) or as having received a special endowment of the Spirit (like medieval priests), two qualities that are out of their reach. Rather, members should regard their pastors as pattern-setters for how they too should live and think. They should heed their life and doctrine and imitate them.

The difference between a member and an elder, though formally designated by a title, is based largely in a difference of maturity, not class. Like a parent with a child, the elder constantly works to call the member *up* and *into* maturity. It is a distinct office, to be sure. And not every mature Christian qualifies. Yet the point remains: an elder strives to reduplicate himself insofar as he imitates Christ (see 1 Cor. 4:16; 11:1).

As a side note, this is one more reason why churches should allow for a plurality of elders. Churches should write "Raise up more elders" into their pastors' job descriptions. Having that plurality gives the church a variety of men to learn from and emulate.

3. *As elders disciple members, so churches make disciples of the nations.* Elders demonstrate loving oversight. Members copy them and learn to demonstrate loving rule. And together they show the nations what loving rule looks like.

A healthy church, then, will produce fathers and mothers who demonstrate for other moms and dads at their children's schools what their own authority should look like. It will produce office managers and

CEOs, senators and judges, engineers and farmers who do the same for people in those fields. Yes, each of these offices possesses its own jurisdiction and responsibilities. But every office—every position of authority into which God places human beings—presents the opportunity to image him in love, obedience, and (for the regenerate) faith.

Churches cannot "transform" cultures or "redeem" cities. Only the gospel word and Spirit can. Nonetheless, they can make disciples, and sometimes make an impact for good on the world around them

I like the character of Atticus Finch in the 1960 novel *To Kill a Mockingbird*. He's not a Christian character, per se. But his view of leadership and authority is certainly Christian. He lived with people in an understanding way. "You never really understand a person until you consider things from his point of view," he remarks, "until you climb into his skin and walk around in it." And he used his power as a lawyer to serve the downtrodden when nobody else in his town would: "The one place where a man ought to get a square deal is in a courtroom, be he any color of the rainbow."[8]

Conclusion

Let's retrace our steps through the eyes of farmer Adam's son. This son spent years watching his father run the family farm. He watched the decent man turn into an angry man, and then into a redeemed man. He saw how the gospel changed his father's way of running the farm. Before coming to faith, his father viewed his workers with suspicion and felt no compunction about overworking them. After his conversion, he built a relationship with them and worked to train them. One of them became a Christian. The others did not, but they grew as honest and competent managers in their own right. No one is entirely impervious to the positive influence of the saints, whether it is accepted or rejected.

Authority well used is humanizing in the most profound ways because God created humanity to rule. The homeless man on the street, the crack dealer, the aborted child, the Nazi soldier, the car salesman, the black youth hanging from a noose, the mother, the teenager, the

8. Harper Lee, *To Kill a Mockingbird*, Perennial Classics (New York: HarperCollins, 2002), 33, 252.

Hollywood starlet—all these he crowned at creation with glory and honor. Each was *meant* to image him.

But the abuse of authority is nearly always dehumanizing. That's authoritarianism. Tragically, we have all taken our call to rule and abused it, thereby abusing others. Why? Because we have loved ourselves more than God.

The solution is simple though challenging: repent of our self-rule and self-love, trust in the death and resurrection of Christ for the forgiveness of sins, and begin to rule on Christ's behalf. Hopefully, we will witness the results of such repentance and rule in our churches, both in our fellowship together and in the overflow of our peacemaking into the outside world.

Conclusion

Good literature, in my experience, captures the human condition in a way a book on doctrine (like this one) cannot. I recall reading one evening a premier non-Christian novelist and a premier Christian theologian back-to-back. The theologian more accurately understood sin. His interpretations were pitch-perfect. Yet the novelist's illustrations of the characters' bondage to sin felt three-dimensional. I stepped into a world. I felt the enslavement. It was like beholding a museum-worthy masterwork in comparison to stick figures.

Admittedly, no piece of literature will illumine the difficult and complex doctrine of God's love fully. Yet certain moments capture one or two aspects, albeit in a mirror dimly. One popular example comes from Victor Hugo's *Les Misérables*. A bishop gives the homeless ex-convict Jean Valjean a night's lodging. Valjean repays the bishop's kindness by stealing his silver candlesticks and sneaking away at night. Police officers capture Valjean and return him to the bishop. The bishop tells the officers that he gave Valjean the silver, sparing him time in prison or worse. Then he whispers to Valjean that, in that act, he has purchased Valjean's soul for God. The rest of the novel demonstrates that Valjean has been transformed by the bishop's sacrificial love. The book's climax is a picture of Valjean himself acting like that self-sacrificing bishop, yet in an even more profound way. For the sake of his daughter and son-in-law, he sacrifices not just silver candlesticks but his life.

I read *Les Misérables* a few months after getting married. I cried for the last forty pages straight. My new wife wondered what was wrong with me until she read it and did the same. What the candlestick scene captures sweetly is the merciful, sacrificial, and redeeming nature of love. The bishop selflessly pardons and blesses a man who is unworthy. Too, the book offers biblical portraits of love and authority. The bishop lovingly uses his position to lift up Valjean. Valjean does the same for his daughter and son-in-law.

That said, I would not argue that this novel captures the holy nature of love, or the exclusive nature of love, or the boundary-drawing nature of love, or love's adamancy for truth, or love's work of judgment, and so on. The bishop lies in order to redeem Valjean. And the character who represents judgment, a police inspector named Javert, is dramatically pitted against love. My book doesn't pack the punch of Victor Hugo's, but I hope I have successfully demonstrated that, if you cannot figure out how love and judgment, or love and authority, or love and holiness work together, you have not yet understood God's love.

A Story about a Community

If we really wanted a story that provided a fuller-orbed picture of God's love, we would need a story about a community. That story might start with a man who, for love's sake, denies himself, stands up, and preaches with authority from the book of God's love, the Bible. He would preach the good news of Christ's holy love. People's hearts would break against this news. They would repent and believe. And they would ask to be baptized into Christ community of love, the church.

Only, that's when the story would get complicated. Each person would bring his or her own backstory into the community. One person's history might involve high school trophies, professional promotions, and a smooth face that masks layers of people-crushing pride. Another backstory might include a childhood of abuse now recycled as abuse toward others, anger endured now anger unleashed. Another person's story, complacency and laziness. Another's, kindness and fear. Hundreds of these backstories would collide and tangle up, like a knot of vines. He offends her. She steps on their toes. They love this teacher. He confronts that group. They struggle with gossip but care for one another. This couple separates. That couple counsels. A young man asks for accountability. A young wife offers a meal. An older woman teaches the younger. An older man evangelizes. This family struggles financially. That family helps. A minority feels overlooked. A majority works hard to empathize. Friendships grow. Generations divide. Truths are declared. Apologies are offered. Words of betrayal. Words of blessing.

In order to present a full-orbed view of God's love, in other words, this story would have to trace out hundreds of plots and subplots. One subplot would demonstrate that love is patient and kind, which of course means that people give one other reason *not* to be patient and kind. Another subplot would show that love does not envy or boast, which, again, presumes temptations to envy and boasting. Still others would reveal that love is not irritable or resentful, does not rejoice at wrongdoing, but rejoices with the truth. The presumption, once more, is that the members of this community continually afford one another reasons to do otherwise.

Yet, little by little, somehow love would shine through the challenges. The obstacles to love would become the occasions for love.

The members of this church would bear all things, believe all things, hope all things, endure all things. Meaning, their life together would not be easy, but difficult. That's what it means to bear and to endure. They would count themselves not emotionally mature and well-adjusted but fainthearted and half-hearted, immature and almost mature, well-meaning and weak. The beginning of love, in fact, would be such honesty about themselves and one another, knowing they remain children still growing into adulthood.

In case you haven't caught it, I'm drawing from what might be the most extended meditation on love in the Bible, the thirteenth chapter of 1 Corinthians. As much as anything, it shows us the love of God—a "love divine, all loves excelling," to borrow a phrase from Charles Wesley. Yet Paul presents it as a way forward for a church, even one rife with division. He calls such love the more excellent way.

A church can display the love of God unlike anything else because of what God has made it. A church is the family of God, which means it experiences something like parental and brotherly love. It is the bride of Christ, which means it's the recipient of an exclusive and tender love. It is the body of Christ, which means members practice loving each other like a person the different parts of his body. It is a holy nation, which points to something like love of country. How many metaphors for the church does Scripture supply? A *flock*, a *vine*, a *temple*, a *people*, a *priesthood*, a *pillar and buttress of truth*, and so on. A church requires all these metaphors to describe its supernatural uniqueness and to embody the many aspects of love.

Displaying God's Love

Fundamentally, the church displays the love of God by loving one another as Christ has loved us: "A new commandment I give to you, that you love one another: just as I have loved you, you also are to love one another. By this all people will know that you are my disciples, if you have love for one another" (John 13:34–35). Christ's love shines in our love for one another. We display him and his gospel.

What does this look like day to day? It looks like a people who share the same mind, have the same love, are in full accord. They strive not to act from selfish ambition or conceit but in humility to count each other more significant than themselves. They look not only to their own interests but also to the interests of others. Most fundamentally, they work to put on the mind of Christ, who, though "in the form of God, did not count equality with God a thing to be grasped, but emptied himself, by taking the form of a servant, being born in the likeness of men," and "humbled himself by becoming obedient to the point of death, even death on a cross." Like him, they "confess that Jesus Christ is Lord, to the glory of God the Father" (Phil. 2:2–11).

Indeed, if we really want a story that provides a fuller-orbed picture of God's love, we don't need a work of fiction. We need a real story about a real community—hopefully your own church. And at the center of this community is a person whose own backstory involved creating the world, coming into the world, living for the world, dying for the world, rising again, and assuming all authority over the world.

God is love, and we behold that love most fully whenever God, who said, "Let light shine out of darkness," shines in our hearts "to give the light of the knowledge of the glory of God in the face of Jesus Christ (2 Cor. 4:6).

Tragically, we place ourselves at the center of the universe. We view ourselves as the center and source of love. Even if we say the words "God is love," we define God and love according to ourselves. Our self-centered love makes its own judgments and imposes its own rule.

Yet God's love is holy. It centers on God, who is triune. It moves outward and inward, like a boomerang. It makes judgments, affirming and denying, including and excluding. It exercises authority, creating and commanding, giving and taking life, building up and tearing down. In these ways, God's love is no different from the love of every sinner and demon. All loves make judgments and aspire to rule. The difference is that the judgments and rule of God's love are always good because he is always good.

Marvelously, God draws sinners like us into the sweep of his triune, God-centered love. So it's not just that God loves us. It's better than that. It's that God incorporates us into his love for himself—"so that the world may know that you sent me and loved them even as you loved me," Jesus prayed to the Father (John 17:23).

We then go to work loving one another, by ruling, subduing, and establishing dominion over a new creation. And in so doing, we are transformed into God's own image from one degree of glory to the next, partaking even of the divine nature.

General Index

Scripture Index

Building Healthy Churches

9Marks exists to equip church leaders with a biblical vision and practical resources for displaying God's glory to the nations through healthy churches.

To that end, we want to see churches characterized by these nine marks of health:

1. Expositional Preaching
2. Biblical Theology
3. A Biblical Understanding of the Gospel
4. A Biblical Understanding of Conversion
5. A Biblical Understanding of Evangelism
6. Biblical Church Membership
7. Biblical Church Discipline
8. Biblical Discipleship
9. Biblical Church Leadership

Find all our Crossway titles
and other resources at
www.9Marks.org

Other 9Marks Books

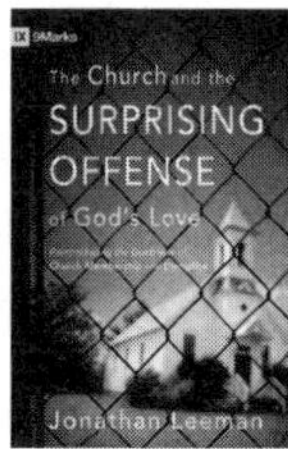

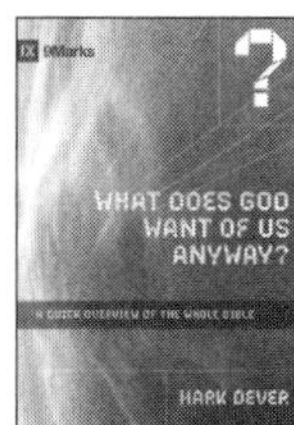

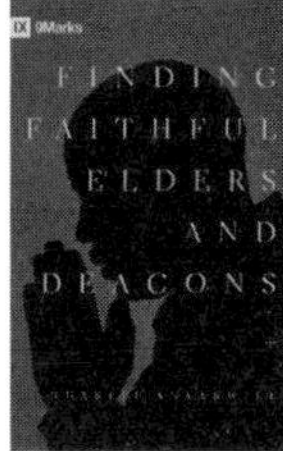

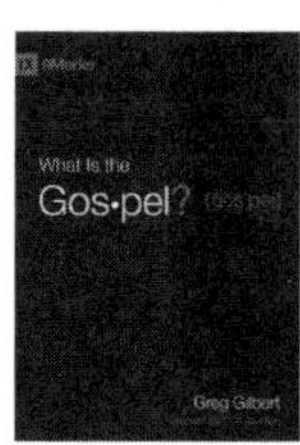

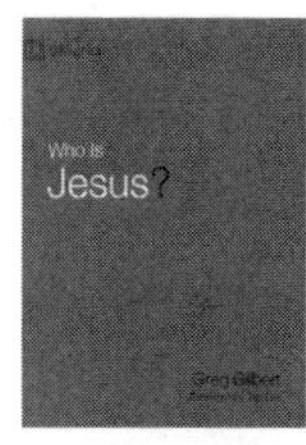

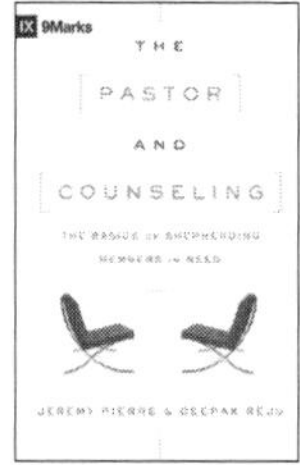

9Marks Series

Building Healthy Churches

Healthy Church Study Guides